How I Recovered

From PTSD
Due to Child Abuse

by David Mindlin

B.M.I., Inc.
Daytona Beach, FL

Copyright © 2014 David Mindlin

Cover photo is from public domain image by Robert & Mihaela Vicol, available at publicphoto.org.

Mindlin, David

How I Recovered From PTSD
Due to Child Abuse

David Mindlin — 1st. ed.

1. Self Help 2. Psychology

3. PTSD 4. Recovery 5. Depression

Publisher: B.M.I., Inc.
P.O Box 214577
S. Daytona, FL 32121-4577

ISBN: 978-0-9913631-0-0

Important–Disclaimer of Warranty Limitation of liability

Warning: I'll repeat this many times throughout the book, because it's true: What I tell you in this book is *my own* experience with PTSD and depression. I'm not a doctor or therapist. Therefore, I'm not recommending that you do anything I will tell you about. I'm just telling you what I did *for myself* in hope that my experience and knowledge may be helpful. And I am recommending that you get the help of a good licensed therapist whenever needed. Also, YOU MUST TAKE FULL RESPONSIBILITY for yourself and how you use or interpret what I tell you about my own recovery. And I expect you to pay attention to all warnings in the book. Therefore author and publisher shall have no liability for how you or anyone else uses or interprets this book.

I am telling you about my experiences so that you may get ideas to design your own unique recovery. I expect you to seek help from a professional when needed, and to take full responsibility for your choices.

The author and publisher shall have neither liability nor responsibility to any person or body or third party for any loss or damage caused or alleged, directly or indirectly, by the contents of this book.

If you can't or don't want to be bound by the above, you can return the book for a full refund. Books or Ebooks can be returned to where you bought them, following their refund policy. If you are using this remedy, your book is unread, and you are having a problem returning, mail documentation to the publisher, who will try to help with your return.

This book is dedicated with love to

my awesome wife,

Beth

Without her, I would not likely have had

a recovery to write about.

Thanks also to old friend Gail Provost Stockwell for advice and support.

And to the training contractors at Lynda.com. Especially David Blatner, Nigel French, Anne-Marie Concepcion, and David Wogahn.

Also thanks to Joel Friedlander for timely advice. I really appreciate any and all help in getting this out and available.

And thanks to Robert & Mihaela Vicol and publicphoto.org for their public domain image, "Black Sea Sunrise", which illustrates recovery very nicely.

Finally, thanks to anyone else who contributed to this book or my recovery in any way.

Table of Contents

Part Five
The Relationships
In Your Life

Introduction

Welcome to what I hope will be a positive, helpful experience for you! I've not only survived severe PTSD and depression from child abuse, I'm much, much happier.

It took me decades to figure out how to do that, and I'm still learning. But I'm lucky. It could easily have turned out *a lot* worse. I wasn't supposed to survive, much less have any happiness. But I did, and feel an obligation to pass on what I've learned.

PTSD and severe depression caused by child abuse are very hard to deal with, because the abuse affects how you see and feel about yourself, how you feel about others, and how you see the world. It happens while you're developing into a person, so it holds back and complicates that development. It leaves you with wounds and problem areas.

That's why they call it "complex" PTSD. These complications are part of you, make you different in some ways from "normal", and are hard to understand. You're left with some difficult feelings and a negative outlook. Combined, these things make it very hard to recover. Since

I succeeded against such great odds, I hope you can benefit from what I've learned.

Here's how I think you can get something useful from this book:

- Take full responsibility for yourself. The truth is, you'll mostly have to help yourself. No one else can do it for you, but you can find information and helpers to help you do the hard stuff. Keep that responsibility even when seeking professional help.

- Be prepared to find out that your abuse was not *at all* your fault. You may not feel that way right now, but you'll find that it's absolutely true. When you really know this, it will mark the beginning of your recovery.

- Know that you will need some good professional help to recover (I will tell you ways to find it), and that it will probably not be easy to find that good help.

- Don't expect to find all your answers here. That's because we're all a little different, and so were our (bad) experiences. But there will be things we have in common, so do expect to find something positive and useful here. If you stay on the positive road, you'll likely find the next thing you need, and the next, and so on, until you have recovered.

- Consider that you may have to read this book more than once to find all that's in it. The book is packed from cover to cover with all I've learned in a lifetime. So allow plenty of time to read and understand it.

- Decide that you will ***not give up***, no matter what. Sometimes that's all that will get you through.

- Expect that there will probably be remnants of PTSD, depression, etc. to manage after you have initially recovered. And that you will be able to manage them. Trust me—70% or 90% better is a life worth living.

- Expect recovery to be a lifelong process—which means things will continue to improve.

Where did the material in this book come from? It came from a lifetime of struggle. First came my psychology studies, and my training and experience as a social worker.

I also read things, heard things, saw things, felt things, tried things, imagined things, survived, hung on, got help, went one step at a time, and figured things out over a lifetime. And I made a lot of mistakes. Out of all that came my recovery.

"You'll Never Get Answers From A Book"

Therapists said that to me more than once. I found it wasn't quite true. When I read self–help books, I was looking for ideas so I could apply my training and experience to come up with my own unique solutions for my recovery. Over more than 30 years, I must have read dozens of books, not counting my psychology and social work training. And looking back, I think I learned more from my social work clients than from anywhere else. They showed me how unique and important we all are, and how often the "labels" just don't fit.

I've forgotten most of the books, as I read most of

them more than 20 years ago. For each 10 books I read, I may have found one idea worth exploring. When I found a promising idea, I first sized it up by applying my training and experience, and I always considered whether a therapist was needed.

In every case, I modified and (for me) improved upon the ideas I found, so they fit me and my life. So what you'll find here is my own unique way of recovering from my own unique problems.

Please assume that whatever I tell you about, including methods or techniques, is my own personal way of doing it, and that *I have done everything mentioned* as part of my own path to recovery. On every page, and in every sentence is what I lived, felt, thought, and did.

And when I use the word "you", remember that I'm telling you about *my* recovery. I mean for you to sift and analyze for yourself whatever I say. You have to come up with your own unique ideas, if you are to recover.

So please don't try to use this or any other self–help book like a cook book. For recovery, you must take the ideas you find and make them uniquely yours, as I did,

I've written this book for you because I think I may be one of only a few who've gained the knowledge in it. I just don't want to take the chance that the knowledge was needed and I didn't do anything.

I sincerely hope you'll get good things out of it, and that your path will lead you to recovery and greater happiness. Best wishes and good luck!

Part One

A successful Recovery: Important First Issues

In this section we'll meet and talk about the first things I had to do or understand to get my recovery going.

Some of these things are: Setting yourself up for success, making important promises to yourself, finding a good helper (a must), and what I did about suicidal feelings.

Chapter One

The Impossible May Be Possible

The young boy was happy, and excited. He was 8 years old. His mom had just called him into the kitchen, and said she wanted to have a little talk, just the two of them. "What nice surprise does Mom have for me?" he wondered. He noticed the weak sunshine of the winter day filtering in the window that morning. All was well.

Then she coldly said the words that would shatter his world forever, and echo down through the years, for the rest of his life: "We've decided to send you away. You're such a bad, terrible boy, and we don't want you here anymore." There had been many other "incidents", but somehow this one was the worst, and hit like a gut–punch.

After begging and pleading in agony for what seemed like the whole day, she agreed that he could stay "a little longer"… "we'll see", but she doubted that he could be good enough to stay for very long. Never again would the boy feel secure in his home, or in himself. From then on, he would always be dreading the day he would be cast out, with no one to care for, or love him.

We move ahead. The boy is now a man in his mid–thirties, with a loving, attractive wife and two wonderful sons. And in his hand he is holding the means to kill himself, and end the pain that seems impossible to bear any longer—the legacy of his abusive childhood. It has been getting really bad lately, and the tortured man feels little hope for relief.

"I want my life back!" he screams again to the empty house. The urge to move the muscles required is very strong, and the muscles tense and let go, tense and let go. Suddenly he imagines his wife and children finding him, the suicide complete. And he cannot bear the thought of doing that to them. He imagines how it will affect each of their lives, and he just can't go through with it. As horrible as his pain is, he can't stand the thought of bringing that pain to those he loves. How long he can go on he doesn't know, but once more, he has defied his destiny.

I was the boy, and young man. I had lived to try one more time to find a way to survive, and maybe even recover from my childhood trauma. Each incident is one of many, and both are absolutely real. Whenever suicide seemed an option, my love for family prevented it.

Believe it or not, I have greatly recovered from the pain, the trauma and all that comes with it, and now lead a mostly normal, happy life. My recovery is not a "cure". My life is usually 80% to 90% better than it was, which seems to me like 1)–a lot, and 2)–enough. I can still be triggered into PTSD, and that is difficult, but I've gained many tools for handling it when it comes up.

My marriage is excellent, and my relationships with my sons and other family are good and rewarding. What's more, I know exactly how I recovered, and I'm able to understand and manage feelings that were once unmanageable. My parents are gone now, but in the last 20–25 years of their lives, we reconciled, and our relationship was very good. I'd say that is a good outcome. I don't think it could have turned out much better for me, and I'm grateful for the good things that have happened!

Why I Wrote This Book

And that's why I've written this book, so that others can learn from my experience, and advance their own recoveries. Having survived, I feel an obligation to share what I learned, for whatever it may be worth.

For many years during and after childhood, I didn't know or understand that what Mom had done had affected me deeply. I noticed I had some trouble socially at times. I suffered from many years of depression. I sometimes didn't behave rationally or appropriately, and had strange or unpleasant feelings. But for many years, the reasons for these things were a complete mystery.

What I finally learned was that I had developed severe depression and "complex" post–traumatic stress disorder due to child abuse.

Good Luck Amidst The Ruins

But I've had some luck. So many of my years were spent just getting through another day. For a long time, forces were pushing me toward a bad end: Breakdown, suicide, giving up. Sometimes just holding my life together was more than I could handle.

It was like going through life carrying an elephant on my back. Somehow, I kept on until I found the way to a better life. Now I'm going to tell you exactly how I did it, in complete detail. Hopefully, you will benefit from my experiences.

Things To Keep In Mind

First, there are some things I'd like you to keep in mind as we go forward.

We're all the same in many ways, and we are different in many ways. Your problems and suffering will not be exactly the same as mine. That's why *you can't just copy everything I did*. I give you this information with the understanding that you'll look at it with a critical eye, and will expect only to find new ideas that you can use to devise your own path to healing and recovery. As I've said, you have to take full responsibility for yourself and your recovery.

Abuse comes in many forms. The abuser may be Mom, or Dad, or both. It may be in the form of beatings, brow–beatings, sexual abuse, or any combination of these. All these situations can produce their own kind of PTSD or severe depression.

Looking back, I've come to think of recovery as being made up of pieces, where the substance of each piece is the same, but for each person, the size, shape, order, etc., of these pieces are unique. So if your kind of abuse is not exactly the same as mine, things you find in this book may help you, too. The recovery you fashion will look a little different from mine, but it will have the same basic ingredients!

Very Important!!

This is not a cookbook, with the single perfect recipe for recovery. *Above all*, please *don't try the ideas or methods I will tell you about alone, with no help*. Some of them are very powerful, and can be dangerous without the guidance of a trained therapist. Some of them deal with your emotional defenses, and you can't mess with them by yourself, or without having something solid to replace them. A good therapist can help you replace them, if appropriate, and keep you safe. If you feel shaky or unsure about an idea or method, pay attention to that feeling. I'll remind you about this many times, because it's important.

It took me a lifetime to go through all the steps to my recovery. I will now tell you all that in as long as it takes to read this book. Even if there's good information here for you, you're not likely to absorb or understand it all for quite some time. You may need a professional just to help you understand some of it, as I have meant for you to understand it. That's why I want to make a condition of my sharing this that you'll handle it responsibly, and get the help you need.

As I'll explain later, finding good help can be hard. This can put us in a difficult spot when we're trying to recover and suddenly seem to be in over our head. In this situation it's important to be realistic, back off, and seek help. I was in this position many times and did just that. Did I always find what I needed right away? No. Did I find it eventually? Most of the time. Do I still have questions sometimes? Yes.

What I Suggest

I'll also suggest you think about making seven promises to yourself (see chapter 2). Some of these promises will take courage to keep. Some will take raw determination, to see it through and not give up. But if you can keep these promises, you'll be ***setting yourself up for success***, and improve your chances of recovery.

What We Will Do

Then I'll show you my own steps to healing and recovery, which will hopefully give you some new ideas for planning your own recovery (I assume you've been working on this already). Some of your work will be very hard, and will take time to accomplish. And for much of your work, you'll need your good helper. I'll suggest how to find one.

Besides explaining jobs I did for recovery, we'll talk about issues with family—especially your spouse and children if you have them. We'll get into how to become a good communicator, and what you and your family can do to help each other.

Finally we'll tackle the question: To reconcile or not to reconcile with your abusing parent(s)? Some will be able to achieve a better relationship, some will not. Hint: The answer is a choice both of you will make, and you can only control your choice. But I'll tell you why as time goes on, you're likely to see things that will change your perspective and make you comfortable with the outcome, whatever it is.

We'll also look at the issue of forgiveness. It's a powerful tool for healing, *BUT* I'll explain why I don't think you should forgive until you're ready, and what it takes to get ready.

A Little About Me

You should know a little about me to help you judge what I tell you. I am in my 70's, with a wife of over 49yrs, two sons, and three grandsons. I hold a BA in Psychology with some advanced study in personality. I spent about 6 years in social work, focusing mainly on child abuse and neglect. I also ran a chemistry lab at a medical research center (and worked at others), after completing many college science, math and engineering courses. From this I gained a strong orientation to the scientific method. My respect for that method should be evident in this book. I've also worked as a computer programmer, and have spent over 40 years as a manager, installer and salesman in our family business. And I've done a little writing.

Perhaps You Can Do It Too

As we begin, I'd like to suggest that, since I was able to recover, perhaps you can too. It's just been a matter of learning what to do, so I see no reason why you can't learn. It was really hard for me to do this, took many years, and sometimes it bordered on the impossible. But I did it, and I don't think there's anything that special about me. I think we all deserve a good life, so why not try?

But let me be very clear about something. It's O.K. if you can't completely recover, and it's O.K. if you have some very difficult times trying. Part of recovery is learning to accept yourself unconditionally, just the way you are. I have a remnant of PTSD, but it's smaller now, and my life is much better. Perfection is not required for happiness!

And it's right to be patient with yourself. In my experience, when you keep trying, things tend to keep getting better over time, in spite of setbacks. You are not competing with me or anyone else, or even with yourself. You are just trying to make your life better and happier, and I believe most people can do that, if they don't give up.

Let me ask you something. Would it be worth it to feel, and enjoy life 50% better? 70%? 90%? However much better things can get for you, isn't "better" a good thing, no matter how much better? My experience is that, however much better your initial recovery improves things, you can keep on learning and getting better as time goes on. As we get older, life gets shorter (and it's pretty short even when you are young). Doesn't it make sense to stick around, try to recover, and see the nice things waiting for you just around the corner?

As I go on now to explain my journey to recovery, I hope it marks a milestone on your own journey, and I wish you my very best!

Chapter Two

Seven Promises

As they say, hindsight is always 20/20. When I look back on my long recovery period, it's easy to see what the obstacles were. Most of them were in my own mind. Many of them were normal defenses we all have. Some were related to persistence, courage, and the ability to handle emotional pain.

I think the obstacles we face with PTSD and depression are common to many other situations in life, and to most people. They are not rare or unique. They may just be a little bigger. I think that means that most of us can deal with these problems, if we will just reach down inside and find what strength we have. I was successful, and I really don't think there's anything that special about me (unless it's that I've been unusually lucky).

Set Yourself Up For Success

In order to set yourself up with an approach and attitude

that's likely to bring success, I ask you to consider making the following seven promises to yourself.

These things were absolutely necessary for my recovery:

- Promise # 1, and the very foundation of recovery:

  I will accept the whole truth about my condition, whatever it is. I will not deny my condition, or blame others for it. Instead, I will take full responsibility, and do my best to handle it (the truth is never as bad as you fear!).

- Promise # 2

  I will learn (with help) the reasons for my negative, self–destructive, self–defeating problem feelings and behaviors. Then I'll learn new ways to deal with them, so they no longer control my life.

- Promise # 3

  I will have the courage to face and deal with the strong, sometimes overwhelming feelings that underlie my condition (with help). Sometimes that will be enough to heal them. When it's not, I will accept these feelings as part of me, so I can learn to control them, and thereby neutralize their negative effects (this is what recovery is).

- Promise #4

  I will find a professional helper who will help me get through the more difficult and dangerous obstacles. I will not give up until I find the right helper for me.

- Promise # 5

  I will learn to adopt new, more positive attitudes and ways of living that will help me toward a better life.

- Promise # 6

  I will learn how to go my own way and live my own life. I will no longer try to be someone I'm not, just to please others. Real love accepts a person just the way they are, and I will do that for myself.

- Promise # 7

  I will not give up until I have kept all the above promises, and have found my own way to recovery and a happier life. No matter how much pain I may feel, or how hopeless it may seem at times. I will not let anything stop me.

I could go into long-winded explanations about each of these promises, but I think you probably get the drift. Recovery is hard work. You have to be honest with yourself, and take full responsibility. You have to try your best. And above all, you must not give up.

The Key To Success

When I was a psychology student, we used to go to a nearby state mental hospital to spend time with the patients. I noticed there were two kinds of patients (they all had very serious illnesses): The kind who kept trying, and the kind who had given up. I never judged those who gave up—how could I know the extent of their suffering, or how hard they had tried? But I noticed that when a patient gave up, it was as though they gave themselves a death sentence. The ones who kept trying were the ones who went home. The ones who gave up usually didn't.

That made a big impression on me, and later on, when I was struggling, I remembered those patients and the lesson they taught me. So I kept trying, and I recovered.

Before we cover the jobs I had to do for my recovery, I want to talk about two important things: How to find a good helper, and how I handled suicidal thoughts and urges.

Chapter Three

Finding A Helper Who Will Help

The advice columnist says it all the time: Get help! Get thee to a therapist or counselor. Sounds simple, but here's the truth: It isn't. Getting good and useful help was one of the hardest things of all.

Of the seven therapists I saw over 30-plus years, only **ONE** helped me in the way I wanted, needed, and expected. All were mainstream professionals. That's a batting average of .140 (not very good). Of the remaining six, one helped in a small but significant way, one did me no harm, and the other four actually hurt me in some way (that would be 57%).

Frustration, Disappointment, And Also Success!

That's not a very good average. I went each time with high hopes and a positive attitude. One told me after one meeting that my problems were "my fault", and I needed extensive therapy. When I said I couldn't afford it right then, he said, "You can't afford not to". Another told me "I don't have much hope for you to get better", and asked my wife "Why did you marry someone like that"? Another told me "We better get working on your career".

When I said I thought I needed to work on the severe depression first, he refused to speak to me any further (the silent treatment turned out to be a trigger for my PTSD). Another, who had agreed to help with medication for a fixed fee, stopped way before the agreed time, saying "I'm going to need some more money right away before I do any more". Another announced that he didn't think there was such a thing as emotional pain. Another just sat there, listening, nodding, grunting, and writing notes, but saying nothing.

I've seen several people go for help with the same result. One was almost killed after reckless medication changes. My family doctor (MD) can't recommend anyone, and thinks they do more harm than good.

Seeking Help Is A Mature, Courageous Decision

It is not easy to make the decision to seek help. To admit you're not in full control of your emotions. It's a mature decision that requires courage. It also requires hope, and some trust that the therapist will be helpful and kind. To make this decision, and have the experiences I did would be enough to make many people give up.

It seems to me that many therapists just don't know enough about this problem to treat it correctly, and in some cases they are just incompetent to help. That's serious, because it can kill you. You will just have to be careful, and pay attention when you feel something is wrong. You can ask your family doctor's advice, or just back away and think it through.

For me, realizing I had a big problem and not being able to find good help was terrifying. It was also very depressing. Worst of all, you really can't fix this by yourself, and you know it.

What to do? There is really no choice. You have to keep looking for good help. Expect it to be hard, frustrating and discouraging. What you *can't* do is give up, or take too much "time out". Ask around. Ask other doctors. And expect to be disappointed a lot. Just don't give up. If I could find what I needed, hopefully you can too. A self–styled "expert" in PTSD and cognitive behavioral therapy MAY be good. Some teaching hospitals have PTSD clinics. And don't overlook your family doctor for medication.

Now I'll give you what I've learned from my own fail-ures, frustrations and successes. I hope it makes finding good help a little easier.

These Things Make Success More Likely

Here's what I would look for in a therapist:

- A person who is professionally trained. A PhD
  Psychologist, a Psychiatrist, or in some cases an
  MSW Social Worker. I have found that Psychologists
  may be best for talking therapy. For medication,
  it *should* be a psychiatrist, but one almost killed

someone I know, so beware. If it seems wrong, act on your feeling. You need a physician who has common sense and a feel for your specific problems. Some family Drs. are great. Look up medications in the PDR and study them, and be careful.

- The therapist specializes in or has successfully treated others for PTSD, or is part of a PTSD clinic.

- The therapist is positive and pleasant. They smile and greet you warmly. They act like they will work with you as a partner/teacher/coach. After a little small talk, they get right down to business. They try not to waste either your time, or your money.

- The therapist seems to respect you.

- The therapist has a procedure for learning about you, and asks what you want from them. Ideally you can find out how they work beforehand.

- It is good if they have you write a personal history, and a list of critical moments in your life for the second session.

- It is good if they ask you to write about your parents, and important members of your family .

- **VERY IMPORTANT**: The therapist assesses and discusses your strengths, as well as your problems. Your strengths form the basis for your healing and recovery, and tell the therapist how fast to go.

- The therapist gives you jobs to do once you are past the assessment stage. This could include reading, writing, or certain exercises.

- The assessment period is thorough, and takes about two one-hour sessions, plus the time you spend at home writing your history.

- The therapist is a good communicator, which means she listens to you and verifies her understanding with you. She teaches you these skills also.

- The therapist brings all her knowledge and training to bear to help you, but makes clear that you are responsible for your recovery, and that it requires hard, steady work.

- The therapist does not push you. You decide that you want to do things, and they help you do them. While discomfort may sometimes be part of therapy, you feel free to raise questions or objections, and know they will be heard.

- The therapist is honest about what she sees, and remains optimistic that you can handle it.

- The therapist does not drag things out. You proceed at the pace you feel is appropriate.

- The therapist tries to be available on the phone for important questions or crises (you should expect to pay extra for significant time, and must realize you are not their only patient).

- If your treatment is not going to either of your satisfaction, and you have discussed this, the therapist refers you to another therapist, giving you a short list of possibilities. The suggested therapists specialize in PTSD.

While a lot of this seems to be only common sense, you may find your therapist does not do these things. You should ask them about any concerns you have. Perhaps they can be worked out. But if you are still not satisfied, you should ask for a referral or make a change yourself.

You should always find out as much as you can about how a therapist works before you see them, although that may not always be possible. You may have to rely on word of mouth or your Family Physician. There are some websites that give this information.

You May Want To Avoid These Things

Now I'll list some things that might ***not*** lead to success:

- The therapist does not have professional qualifications. Or they seem very attached to a particular school of thought, and you feel they are a little extreme about it.

- Something about the therapy sounds strange. People on the fringes can be disturbed themselves, or have an agenda that they want to make you part of. They may appeal to your wish to deny, or blame others. This type is very likely to do you harm. Stay with science and the main stream.

- The therapist does not seem to like or respect you

- The therapist has no particular assessment procedure—you just dive in.

- The therapist has you tell about all your problems,

but never explores your strengths or the good things in your life. This can lead them to develop a warped picture of you, and to think you are more seriously ill than you actually are.

- The therapist does not seem to understand what you are telling them, and does not verify his assumptions with you.

- The therapist assumes a lordly attitude: "I am the doctor!" Etc. You feel more like a peon than a partner.

- The therapist does not share with you what he sees. He seems to be manipulating instead of sharing.

- The therapist hardly says a word–OR–talks on and on about things that have no meaning for you.

- You don't seem to get along well with the therapist on a personal level.

- The therapist is not too available for questions.

- The therapist will not refer you elsewhere if your work together is not progressing.

These are **not** hard and fast rules for everyone. But they are the sum of what I learned after many experiences. When you think about it, most of them are just plain common sense. We should never forget that the purpose of therapy is to help the patient or client.

You have the right to ask about and understand the method of treatment. You have the right to expect that, if the therapist can't help you, they will try to do you no harm, and will refer you to someone who may be able to work with you better.

You Have A Right To Do What's Best For You

In short, you have the right to pursue what you believe to be your own best interests so you can heal and recover. If you don't feel you are getting what you need, and have discussed this with your therapist, and do not get a satisfactory explanation, I think you should consider not wasting further time, energy or money there. You could move on and find another therapist you think may help. What you should *not* do is become discouraged and give up, even for a "little while". Doing so will waste part of your life.

If I could heal and recover from my problems, surely anyone can. Remember, over 50% of my therapists hurt me somehow, and only 25% helped. If I hadn't found good medication and two good therapists, I'd hate to think what would have happened. And I found these things by **NOT GIVING UP**.

It can be a jungle out there when you're looking for help. But you really have no choice. *The road to recovery requires a professional helper*. You can't do it by yourself, no matter how smart and tough you are. So if you have to go through a few turkeys to find the golden goose, that's just how it will have to be. You have to accept the responsibility for keeping on, and for doing the right thing. Then your good helper, when you find them, can guide you through the minefields to healing and recovery.

Things To Do While Looking

First, if you feel suicidal, you must get help *right*

now! Even average help will probably work.

Next, you can try positive things that you think may help, as long as they don't make things worse. Here are some things I did:

I learned about positive mental attitude, and it helped a lot.

I got more exercise, which also helped.

I discussed medication with my family doctor, and we tried one that worked, and which I still take today.

I tried to always do what I understood to be the right thing. That really made a difference.

I tried some of the less dangerous things I'll tell you about later. This helped too.

In short, I did anything I could find or think of that might be positive and helpful. I didn't sit around waiting for someone or something to save me. And that's what you have to do—keep looking and keep trying to help yourself.

I hope my personal guidelines to finding a good therapist will be helpful, and save you time, money and frustration. Just use your good sense, and trust your feelings about it as a consumer. You *do* have a right to get the help you need, and you *will* find it if you just don't give up!

Cognitive Behavioral Therapy

Right now (2013), science is telling us that Cognitive Behavioral Therapy (CBT) is the most effective one for treating PTSD and depression. I've just recently learned about it, and have found that some of the methods I came up with over the years are part of or compatible with CBT. It has one big advantage, in that some texts say you can do it by yourself (unless you find you need help). I think that's because it involves learning about your thoughts and beliefs, which are more or less on the surface.

How It Works

CBT says that what you believe about an event effects how you think about it, and can cause errors in how you think, which can in turn lead to things like anxiety, anger and fear. Also your need for control and certainty can fuel beliefs that cause painful thoughts and emotions.

For example, you may perceive someone has been inconsiderate, and you may react indignantly with much anger, because what they did was "wrong" (belief) and "unfair". This, in turn, causes strong anger, anxiety, etc., which continues. In reality, you can't control what others do. CBT calls this a toxic thought pattern that you can change.

It says that by examining your beliefs and thought patterns, you can make changes that improve your life. It also says that you have to stop avoiding the things that upset you, and learn to approach and feel more realistically about them.

It says that by changing thought patterns, you can change how you feel, because most (not all) feelings come from thoughts.

I Agree, Mostly

I think CBT could help most people with PTSD and other problems. But I need to point out one thing: In my understanding, when PTSD activates, the strong feelings don't come from thoughts, but from a connection in your mind between past abuse events and an event that's happening now. It's both instant and automatic. It would be *after that* when CBT's feelings–from–thoughts would be true.

I recommend you explore CBT to see how it might help. There are many books available, and I found the "For Dummies" series (CBT and CBT workbook) as good as anything.

Now we'll talk about a sensitive subject: The urge to suicide, and what you can do about it.

Chapter Four

Suicide: Things You Need To Know

As told earlier, I held the instrument of my death in my hand many times, just inches and seconds from ending my life. At those times, I was experiencing an overwhelming *urge* to kill myself. This urge is hard to believe or understand for those who've never felt it, but those who have know exactly what I'm talking about. How could someone passionately desire to kill himself? How, indeed?

If you've experienced the urge to suicide, you know how serious, strong and dangerous it can be. The word urge is very appropriate, because it's a powerful, overwhelming desire, in the same league with sex or eating and drinking. If you haven't felt this, it's very, very hard to understand.

Where Does This Come From?

First, let me be clear that **there are other driving forces besides the ones I will talk about**. Loss of a relationship or what feels like unbearable shame or failure are two examples.

This is only about PTSD/child abuse, though some of this may apply to other causes. These are my ideas.

With that in mind: First, there may be hidden anger or rage—something that I think all victims of child abuse feel. This develops because it's too dangerous to express anger created by the abuse toward the abusing parent. So it is choked back and hidden in the unconscious mind, where it remains.

There may also be a passionate self–hate, and that develops from the abusing parent's seeming hatred of the abused. The young child accepts it is "my fault", and learns in this way to hate himself. Later pain, failure, etc. are felt to be "my fault", and the victim comes to hate himself with a passion. *The victim actually takes on, or "identifies" with the abuser's apparent hate*, and feels responsible for all that has happened to him. Usually this is hidden, but under stress, it can suddenly appear in the form of suicidal urges. At this time the hidden anger is added to the hate and turned inward, and the victim feels the full force of both. This is a very deadly combination!

With each bout of depression, each perceived failure, the pressure toward suicide can grow. Things seem more and more hopeless. The victim feels more and more help-less to change things for the better. At some point, suicide can *seem* to be a good choice.

There Is A Way Out

But what if the victim learns and comes to believe that it is not "their fault"?

And what if she finds a safe way to reach and examine the anger/rage hidden in her subconscious mind? Then there wouldn't be anything fueling the urge to suicide, and the victim could come to realize that they *do* have the power and ability to change their life for the better. That's pretty much how, with help, I disarmed my suicidal urges.

But You Must First Get Help

Let me make something very clear. ***Never attempt to handle suicidal urges by yourself. That is impossible***! You ***must*** find a good helper for this, and even a mediocre one can do the job. Do not wait or hesitate, because suicidal urges are an ***emergency***. They are very dangerous (more than anything else we will talk about), and you should treat them as such.

You can't heal or recover or reclaim the happiness you deserve if you are dead.

I had reached the point where I not only knew how I would do it, but had the means in my hand—several times. I realized the danger and went right to a therapist (the one who helped me in a significant way, but did not pan out otherwise). He was able to get across that it wasn't my fault, and that was enough to stop it.

Things That Contribute To Suicidal Urges

Now I want to go into a little more detail about the things I think contribute to the urge to suicide, so you can better understand it. First, let's talk more about what drives the suicidal urge.

Picture an infant who cries for some reason. Then let's say the parent, following their need to control the infant, does not answer until they choose to. The infant will sense there is no one there when they need someone, and will eventually give up. They learn that they can't trust the parent. Then, picture this child between the ages of one and three. His needs are still ignored, and if he shows anger or aggression, he is severely punished, sometimes in a frightening way. He will sense there is deadly danger in these behaviors, due to the violence of the response.

Anger and aggression serve many positive purposes in a young child. The anger creates space for the child to exist as an individual. The aggression promotes exploration of his world, and helps establish a "me". Nurturing parents tolerate these emotions unless they become extreme. Abusing parents do not respond normally to infant needs, and do not tolerate the child's anger and aggression.

They basically frighten the child into submission, using loud shouting and their greater physical strength. Sometimes this escalates into severe physical abuse, or even death. The child rightfully fears for his life, and the lesson about not trusting is reinforced. So what can the child do with their anger? It is not safe to show it. So it gets buried, swallowed, or "repressed", as they say in psychology. It is still there, and that's the anger that comes out to haunt you and mess up your life when you get older.

As for the aggression, this normal behavior is also repressed, and that's why abuse victims have so much trouble "finding themselves" when they become adults. It's not safe to be yourself, you have to please others and be someone else (sometimes upon penalty of death!). But you can't do that either, because you can only be you. You can't win.

With suicidal urges, this anger and aggression is turned against the self because of another thing that happens to abused children:

The abusing parent is always saying terrible things to their child: "You are bad. You are no good. You are worthless. You make me sick. You are a lazy bum. The word 'shit' comes up a lot. King shit. You pile of shit. I wish you were never born. I hate you. I'll kill you if you…". Believe it or not, this really hurts! And you hear it day after day, year after year. From the time you are able to understand English.

You Believe What They Told You

Now here's the really ironic part. This doesn't stop you from needing or loving your parent. In fact, you see them as a kind of all–knowing and all–powerful god. So if they say these things, they must be all true. So you come to ***believe these things about yourself***, and come to hate yourself, because you are just so damned rotten. And to top it off, you believe that this is somehow your fault!

When you put together this self–hate and the buried anger and aggression, you have a cocktail called suicidal urges. It's very powerful, very passionate, and very dangerous.

But that's not all. Say you've been experiencing depressions that last weeks, or even months. And say this has been happening for years, and nothing you have tried will stop it. Not only that, it's been getting worse as time passes, and your former optimism and courage is slowly turning into hopelessness and despair, which of course makes the depression worse.

Now put that together with the rest of the cocktail, and imagine trying to live a life like that.

Sound far–fetched? Well, welcome to my life (some of the time), as I lived it from birth until about age 52, when I discovered modern antidepressants, and later, when I finally was able to fit all the pieces together. And I know I'm not the only one.

When you think about what is stacked against the abuse victim who is feeling suicidal urges, you can see why I say it is impossible to handle it by yourself. There's nobody that smart or tough in the whole world. You *must* get *immediate* help if you find yourself in this situation.

Whew! But I Survived!

Now think about the other side of the coin. I experienced all this and more, **BUT** *I survived it all*. Not only that, but I healed the buried anger, and recovered to great extent from PTSD and severe depression. Now, I don't think there is anything that special about me. If I can do it, maybe anyone can. Maybe you can!

How will the therapist help you? It will depend on your personal situation, but they will likely focus on the self–hate. They may have you go back in time in your mind to when the abuse was taking place and help you to re–live some of it. The idea is to help you *experience why what happened to you was wrong, and that you didn't deserve it*, to the point that you can believe it. When you are successful with this, it will be possible for you to learn to love yourself–an important part of recovery.

Love Can Keep You Alive

Before I move on, I want to tell you about something that kept me alive. Each time I was ready to pull the plug, I thought about my beloved wife and children finding me afterward. And I just could not do that to them. I love them too much. So I came to see that I had no choice but to keep trying, until I either succeeded or blew into a million pieces. It was love that kept me alive. Maybe you have someone you can spare from that bad experience too. It's a good thing to focus on, as you disarm your suicidal urges and move on to healing and recovery.

Get that help *now*! Take any medication that is prescribed (after looking up the side effects), and keep fighting until the urges stop completely. And go back if they start up again! Life is pretty short as it is, so why miss out on the really good part that may be just around the corner?

Now I want to talk about the main thing that keeps

people from healing and recovery. Hint: Are you a queen (or king) of denial?

Part Two

Obstacles To Overcome
What Abuse Does To You

In this section we'll talk about the greatest obstacles to recovery: Denial and other defenses that ordinarily help us, but not in this case.

Then I'll show you what abuse does to a person, which explains why we feel as we do, and why we look at ourselves and the world the way we do.

Chapter Five

Denial–An Enemy Of Recovery

"There's nothing wrong with me," "I'll be O.K.", "It'll go away", "The doctors will just mess me up, No way am I taking an antidepressant". Sound familiar? When we say these things to ourselves, we may be feeling fear. And we are *denying* reality.

A Normal Defense That Can Stop Recovery

Denial is a way we defend ourselves against unpleasant thoughts. If we ignore it, maybe it will go away. If you were a normal person without any emotional disorders like depression or PTSD, denial might actually work! Minor problems sometimes do go away by themselves. But with severe disorders, there's no way it will work. Since we're wired to use these defenses, we use them, even if it means they will trap us and keep us from getting better.

For people with disorders, defenses can be the thing that *prevents* healing.

Why We Deny

So why do we deny? In a word: Fear.

Partly, we're afraid that if we admit there is something very wrong, we will fall apart completely and forever. We're also terrified of what will happen if we give up control to a therapist (in the right kind of therapy, you keep control and responsibility for yourself).

But the thing we fear most is that the abusing parent was right about us: We are "no good", "unworthy", hopelessly flawed. *If we admit there is "something wrong" with us, it means they were right*! And deep down the abuse victim believes they were right. So we refuse to face there is even a problem. We also tend to deny the fact and extent of our abuse, making excuses for the abuser, and "forgetting" what happened, the feelings it caused, and how it impacted our lives.

You will never heal or recover if you can't get past denial. Do you do this? Are you afraid to face the truth? The truth is never as bad as you think. Do you make excuses for the abuser? Do you avoid remembering what actually happened? I did these things.

Watch Out For This One!

Warning: *On the outer fringes of therapy there are those who push "repressed memories", often dealing* *with supposed sexual or other abuse that the supposed victim can't remember. This type of "therapist" has a personal agenda, and will keep making suggestions, and get you to "remember" such supposed incidents. Problem is, once these people get through with you, you can't tell the difference between reality and their suggestions. You will think that the suggestions are real, even if they are not. To keep this from happening to you, don't let a therapist push or suggest anything, and be skeptical about "repressed memories".*

The latest scientific research suggests that memories of trauma may be "fragmented", and not the same as normal memories. It's thought that trauma memories are not integrated into normal memory, but are lying around in little pieces somewhere in the brain. I don't know about the exact truth of this, but I can tell you that in my experience, we do sometimes deny or repress such memories, and they are very emotionally charged.

All I can say is that I had no problem remembering, on my own, exactly what happened, when I wanted and was ready to. The only help I ever had with this was an exercise where you imagine the abuser sitting in an empty chair across from you, and tell them what you want to say. There were no suggestions made at all by the therapist.

Research also suggests that "fragmented" memories can be put together out of context, and the result will seem like a real memory. Also, it says that completely false memories can be "planted" by the suggestions of the therapist, and they will seem like a real memory. Experts warn against any form of suggestion, including hypnosis.

I think real memories will come on their own, without a suggestion being made. Some families have been badly hurt, even torn apart because of "repressed memory" therapists. Their spiel may be seductive, and seem to be an easy way out. But their way is a trap that will only add to your misery.

Another Roadblock: "It's _____'s Fault"

There is another defense that can get in the way of healing, called projection. In this defense, you may blame others for your problems, *but not the ones really responsible —the abusing parent(s)*. You may blame a brother or sister, or a spouse for what the abusing parent did. This is most likely to happen when you have mixed feelings about the abusing parent.

So you shift blame for the bad feelings to someone else. This is another trap that will stop your recovery. If you believe it's someone else's "fault", then you have no control, and are stuck. To move forward, you'll have to face who really hurt you.

Defensive Gymnastics

You may be getting the idea that we sometimes perform incredible emotional gymnastics to avoid the truth, usually out of fear. This is *absolutely true*! But when we do this, we make it impossible to heal or recover. You can't survive on lies for long. It just gets harder and more painful. The sooner you summon the courage to face your problems honestly, the sooner you will succeed at healing and recovery. And you will likely need professional help to get past denial.

The Truth About Us

You may get from this that in a way, we are emotionally weak, or why would we need these defenses? You would be right. In fact, "macho" is a defense against the weakness that is there. One weakness we have is that we can only take so much fright, abuse, etc. as children, before we either resort to defenses or crack up. Yes, we can be tough, and we can be strong, but at times we can be in a situation that we're just not up to handling.

The times we can't handle something are either in childhood, when we are relatively helpless and dependent, and lack adult skills for handling things, or in adulthood, when we graphically see or are imminently threatened by death. It is these times that come back later to haunt us. Some things that happen in child abuse, no child could possibly handle.

Yet we somehow feel we "should have". That comes from looking back at childhood through adult eyes. There is no shame for a child to be a child, and have the innocence and vulnerability of a child! To really understand these feelings, you have to learn to look at what happened through "child eyes". That's something a good therapist can help you do.

Defenses in a normal person buy time to come up with something better, or allow them to dismiss the problem as not important enough to clutter up their life right now.

In people with emotional disorders, defenses can be a desperate attempt to avoid the truth, and a major roadblock to healing and recovery. In the case of child abuse, a childhood defense may be to bury feelings, like anger, that could get you killed if you expressed them. That makes perfect sense at the time, but these feelings will haunt you in adulthood. They stay buried and don't go away, and pop up from time to time.

My Own Fight With Defenses

In my case, there were times I couldn't admit I had a problem. It was my wife's fault, or that person's fault over there. Or, the problem was over—"everything's O.K. now that I feel better". At those times, I was unconsciously and desperately defending myself from what I feared was the awful truth—I was permanently flawed, inferior, no–good. And those untrue fears were keeping me locked in chains, unable to recover!

IMPORTANT!!

We will always have and use these defenses, because they are wired in, and we can't live without them. So abuse victims who have PTSD and depression have to, with help, sort through the ones holding them back, and replace them with something that works better. Again, I say *don't try to do this by yourself*. Your defenses hold you together, and if you mess with them and don't know what you are doing, you can put yourself in real danger. **A THERAPIST IS A MUST HERE.** A good therapist will know how much you can take at a time, and will not push you harder than you can take. They will also know what you need to replace your faulty defense with, and will help you do it. ***Trying to remove a defense yourself would be like removing a structural element from a house–it could come crashing down***. A professional contractor would not let that happen, and neither will a good therapist.

But the more you know about your defenses, the faster and smoother therapy will go. So now we'll talk about them in more detail. Let's look closer at the fears behind them.

A Closer Examination Of Defensive Fears

I remember those fears well. We all are afraid of being different, and not being accepted by others. Well, the feelings that come from being abused make you feel different. So you do your best to hide it. To admit you have a problem and need help would be an admission of being different. So you may deny, and blame others for your feelings. And to admit something is "wrong" can mean to you that your abuser was right about what they told you: That you are no good.

There is also a fear of loss of control. You believe if you go for help, someone will take over, and may force you down a path you do not want to travel. You also feel that going for help is an admission that you have lost control, and that is frightening and humiliating. In fact, you may have a general fear of your feelings, and what they may make you do. *This fear may intensify if you do go for help*. That's normal. In therapy these feelings tend to become stronger and more numerous at first, because 1.) you've been avoiding them, and 2.) you are now noticing and focusing on them. This intensity does ease off with time.

Fear of admitting there is "something wrong" with you can lead you to lash out and blame those close to you for your bad feelings (spouse, children). If you can believe that your problem is "out there" somewhere, you can maintain the delusion that you are perfectly normal. Then, if you do lash out and blame spouse or children, what may follow is guilt (which leads to lower self–image), and the fear that your family will abandon you, which you ironically promote by blaming them unfairly.

As you can imagine, these fears and defenses only make the problems worse, and keep you from getting the help you need. I experienced all of the above fears and more, and they are ***normal*** for a person who has been abused and has a disorder as a result. I think many therapists don't realize that their first task is to help the victim through these fears and defenses, where they are present, and praise the courage and maturity of the person who comes to them burdened not only by the abuse, but also by the fear of what it "means" about them.

There will certainly be no healing or recovery if these first issues are not addressed. My advice for the abuse victim with a disorder is to face these fears with the knowledge that healing and recovery are possible, even likely. And know that there is no shame in being a victim. There is pride in a determined effort. You will need to summon courage to seek the help you need, and especially to go on when you are not satisfied with the help you're getting.

In that case, remember: You are worth finding a good helper, and deserve to heal and recover.

The Fears Are Untrue—And It Was Not Your Fault

Never were the fears I had true. It was never as bad as I thought or felt. In fact, I was actually a pretty good person. It pays to have the courage to do what is right for yourself, and I'm a living example that this is true.

What you will find when you let go of the fears and defenses, and admit to your problem, is that the abuser was wrong when they told you you're bad. You are not bad, and are just as good as anyone else. You will find the abuser was projecting their bad feelings onto you. They had a problem, and used you to "solve" it. You were a scapegoat, a stand–in for someone else who hurt them. A punching bag. They used you in a very bad way.

Now let's get real: While the abusing parent(s) were probably not facing or fully aware of what they were doing, that doesn't excuse what they did. It is something they should be sorry about and apologize for. Adults are always fully responsible for their actions, and should accept responsibility if they hurt their children. Further, they are responsible for loving and nurturing their children so they grow up to physical and emotional good health. Children are **not** responsible for the abuse their parents commit on them. They don't "deserve" it, did not "ask for" it. All children deserve to be loved and valued as individuals. All children, no exceptions.

It was the abusing parent's fault, not yours. The pain you suffer was caused by their actions, and you were not responsible for it. Facing these facts does not mean you will have to hate your parents forever. But you *must* face the facts to heal and recover. You must acknowledge the abuser's responsibility for the abuse, for the way it has made you feel, and for the damage it has done to your life. And that your responsibility is to now take charge, and do all you can to heal and recover from what was done to you.

When You're Ready, Time To Remember

Part of preparing for things like getting in touch with anger and "standing up" (see later) is remembering the major incidents of your abuse. This is a painful process that will take some time. And the time to start this is after you have conquered any defenses getting in the way. That's how I did it.

If, as I'd recommend, you use a good helper to help get through this difficult stage, remember that there must be no suggestions by the therapist, no hypnosis, etc., as I've already explained.

When you can get past denial and find a good therapist, you're ready to work on the issues that are causing you pain. Now we'll discuss some issues that may come up on your journey to healing and recovery.

Chapter Six

What Abuse Makes You Feel

Again she wore her mask of hate as she screamed the same awful words, insults and accusations. A foam of spittle came from her mouth as she "spanked" him and screamed at him for what seemed like forever. "I am such a hopelessly bad child", he thought, feeling more low and miserable with each painful blow. This happened over and over again, day after day, year after year.

Being abused over a long period of time has a profound, negative effect on how you feel about yourself. Remember, it usually starts when you're born. You can be under siege right from the beginning, and you are certainly not equipped to defend yourself. How could a baby or toddler or small child fight back, or stand up for himself? How could a child of any age? What chance do you really have in that situation? From birth you receive blow after blow after blow, year after year after year. Pow! Pow! Pow! You must simply absorb it, let it affect you as it will, and try to survive it. And you can't fight back!

First, The Good News

I think there are some differences in how it affects people, and I can only talk about how it seemed to affect me. *I want to make clear that abuse doesn't destroy every part of you. There are areas where you are strong.* For instance, my intelligence was always praised, so I felt strong in that area, and did well in school. Also, I have always been a stubbornly independent person and thinker, and that has helped me a lot. It is your strong points that anchor your recovery. So as we talk about negative effects of abuse keep in mind your strengths, and that ***these strengths will help you recover***.

How Abuse Changed Me

One casualty for me was parts of my self–image. Let's see how that could be.

From early childhood, I was severely controlled. As a baby, I was ignored when I cried (I know this because my mother bragged about it). For the slightest infraction (real or imagined), I was screamed at, spanked frequently with gusto, and told I was bad. One of my earliest memories is of my mom screaming at me in a rage, with that horrible face, that I'd better "toe the line", or else. I remember particularly being called "king shit" a lot.

A good example of this control was at about age 3. I had gone to a local store with a friend and his mom. They all got an ice cream cone, and got one for me. I refused to eat it because my mom hadn't given me permission, and walked home with the ice cream dripping down my arm. I was terrified to eat it because of what would happen if I did. I can remember being in fear of something or other like that most of the time. When you are afraid to eat an ice cream cone at that age, you are under pretty tight control!

The messages I was getting were that I was bad the way I was, and needed to become someone else: Whoever and whatever I was told to be. Also that I was a "bad seed", unworthy of love. In this situation, no matter how hard you try to please, you can never win. How can you change what you are? And as this goes on, you come to believe what they say about you. They are all–knowing, all–powerful gods. You are just a little child. What do you know? So you accept it as fact that you are bad, unworthy. That belief is common to most abuse victims.

As I told you earlier, the clincher came for me at age 8, when my mom said, "We've decided to send you away." At that moment, I felt something break in me that would never quite be fixed. I can remember everything in the room, the time of day, the light in the room, what season it was, the temperature, everything. Like life just stopped dead still. And it still hurts to think about it over 60 years later. I remember sobbing, begging, and feeling pain and panic beyond belief.

And my mom, after talking about some of the places they could send me, after torturing me for a long time, said that they might think about holding off "today". "We'll see", she said. But she made it clear she didn't think I would be able to be good enough, that I was really just too rotten to be allowed to live there any more. Actually, I think I was a pretty good kid, but I didn't believe it then. To me, this was a violent emotional shock. Before it, I felt some security even with the ongoing abuse. After, I felt absolutely no security, ever again.

Home, Yet Often Feeling Homeless

Of course after that, I was only allowed to have a home by mom's good graces, which I seemed to be out of most of the time. From then on I knew that I was at best being tolerated, but that I didn't have a real home. I felt sure I wasn't loved. I was an outcast waiting to be cast out. Sometimes I forgot about it, but then something would remind me.

Later, as a teenager, absolutely *nothing* I did was right. I was met at the door every day with a bawling out, punishments, lists of infractions. Once I was told to get a job (for the summer) "today, or don't bother coming back" (fortunately, I guess (?), I got a job). When I was big enough, mom took to slapping me hard across the face. One day I grabbed her wrist as she was doing it and said "You're not going to do that to me any more". I was severely punished by both parents for "touching" my mother, but she never did it again.

I'm not telling you this for your sympathy, but to show you (if you don't already know) what being abused is like. So you can get a perspective on what it could do to a person.

Would it shock you to learn that I have had a lifelong fear of being abandoned? Or that I've often found excuses not to do what I really want to, and instead have tried to figure out what others want me to do (to the point of ruining my working life)? Or that I've had trouble being able to feel good about myself? Those things would follow logically from what happened to me, wouldn't they? And that's pretty much how it works. ***There are good reasons for why we feel and behave the way we do***. In order to heal and recover, we just have to understand these reasons.

Things Abuse Can Make You Feel About Yourself

- If you are told by the "gods" you are bad, worthless, rotten, or some four letter version of the above, ***you will believe it***, especially if no one else tells you different.

- If you are threatened with abandonment, you will probably not feel secure from then on.

- If you are told that what you are is not acceptable, you will probably try to "become" someone else, who might be O.K. And you will not be able to do it.

- If your instincts and judgment are constantly criticized, you will probably not trust yourself.

- If what you want to do is constantly criticized, you will probably not aggressively seek it, and will not feel your life is your own. You may then spend your whole life trying to "find yourself".

- If you are not allowed to express anger, you will not

learn how to stand up for yourself, and may find your anger turned within, against you.

- If you feel hated and outcast, you will hate yourself.

- If what you do is never good enough, you will come to believe that no matter how hard you try, it will never be good enough.

- If your parents do not love you in the way you need to be loved, you will feel unlovable.

- If you are threatened with death, either directly or subtly, you will believe it. This fear will underlie all the other bad feelings, and give them greater urgency.

- Due to the other feelings already mentioned, you may feel like a fraud, waiting to be exposed.

- You may fear getting too close to others, because if you do, they will see how bad you really are.

- You may feel the world is a hostile, dangerous place.

- You may be waiting nervously for the next bad thing to happen.

- You may have a tendency toward paranoia (after all, someone really *was* out to get you since you were born).

- You may be expecting a really bad thing to happen to you, like cancer.

And this is only a partial list of the fruits of child abuse. It is my own personal list. It's clear that for every one of these bad feelings or fears mentioned, there is a solid connection to what actually happened to me.

There is a good reason for everything you feel (and that may include a problem with brain chemistry).

Cause And Effect

Isn't it obvious, when you think about it, that abuse is likely to cause depression? Who could withstand all this fear and bad feeling forever? Of course, you don't feel these things all the time. You are able to live and have some fun. But these fears and bad feelings will keep popping up, and with time, depression becomes more and more likely, until something happens to trigger it off. PTSD is less understood, but is always connected to fear of death. Who is more helpless and vulnerable to death threats (real or implied) than a small child?

And isn't it obvious that all this being done to you will eventually create in you a negative, fearful, pessimistic state of mind? I think there's really nothing mysterious about this. You get abused regularly, and it will make you feel certain things about yourself and the world around you.

A Negative Frame Of Mind

One effect of abuse is a negative mental attitude. I remember that most of my childhood daydreams would turn out bad. If bad things keep happening, and you expect more of the same, it's quite impossible to be an optimist. As we'll see later, a negative attitude brings more bad things! I'll tell you how to change that later.

It Stays In Your Head

One thing was shocking once I realized it. The bad things your abuser tells you stay in your head, and become a part of you. I knew this as a student of psychology, that your parents' voices become part of you (Freud called it the superego, Berne and Harris called it the Parent). But to realize I kept telling myself I was unworthy, bad, useless, didn't deserve what I wanted, etc. was still a shock. I found it was so ingrained that I created a happiness notebook to help me spot when I did this. I found that I could change my thinking by being more aware of what was going on.

You Can Change It

Your job is to reverse the bad programming by the abuser, and to train yourself to feel good about yourself, to be proudly who you are, and to learn where your parents taught you wrong, and how to see things the way loved children do. And you must learn how to have a more positive outlook (Cognitive Behavioral Therapy is a way to do this).

I'm here to tell you it can be done, enough to let you enjoy life more, because I did it!

Soon, I'll share more ideas as to how it can be done. Now we'll look at how being abused affects your feelings about others.

Chapter Seven

Abuse And Relationships

Mom and Dad were home, and had just told their four–year–old boy to go outside and play. The boy was scared, and said he didn't want to go. They asked why, and he told them what had happened the day before. Two older, much bigger girls had come into the neighborhood and had beaten him with tree branches, and he was afraid it would happen again today. They insisted he had to go out, and when he cried, they dragged him down the stairs, pushed him outside, and locked the door. As he begged to be let back in, he saw them go up the stairs, laughing at him.

I was told many years later that they were "teaching me to be a man", and that they later found me in a neighbor's house, where I had found refuge. Lucky for me those girls never came back. Is it surprising I had issues with *trust* and *betrayal* after that and other similar incidents?

If you come out of your home feeling bad, unworthy and insecure, it's not a good foundation for building relationships with others. When you don't feel good about yourself, it can show in many ways, large and small.

We all have problems with relationships, but being an abused child makes these problems much harder to handle. It's not just that there are always some other children looking for weakness to exploit to "solve" their own problems. It's that *your whole attitude and way of looking at others is changed by your abuse*. That's how it was for me.

Relationship Problems Caused By Abuse

Trust and betrayal are big issues for the abused. It will be much harder for you to trust other people. And you may be more fearful of, and sensitive to betrayal than is normal. These things can make you seem overly sensitive or hard to get along with.

You will be more sensitive to bullying and aggressiveness, which makes you more attractive to bullies. This can make you feel worse about yourself, and add to the stress and tension in your life, as if there isn't enough already.

You are likely to have trouble with the emotions of anger and fear. You may impress others as being overly fearful or emotionally unstable, which will tend to drive them away. This can cause trouble for making and keeping friends. If you have this problem, it will also make you feel worse about yourself.

You will probably be very sensitive to *criticism, cruelty and teasing*. This can further isolate you. You will be especially sensitive to these things coming from an authority figure, like a teacher, supervisor, or boss.

When the time comes for adolescent and adult love relationships, you may have problems for all the above reasons, including new stronger than normal fears of rejection and abandonment. Issues of trust, betrayal, fear and anger, and the appearance of emotional instability may become even more intense. Adolescence is a hard time for everyone. For the abused child, it's worse.

Abuse Sets You Up For More Problems

As you can see, being abused from an early age *sets you up for social failure and abuse by others*. You come out of your abusive home with a pre–arranged low spot in the pecking order of social relations. Then, your abuse is strongly reinforced in the outside world. The feelings that you are bad and unworthy are further strengthened by the experiences you have been set up to have. Until you are able to take control of this, there will tend to be a downward spiral of self–esteem, and some troubles in social relationships.

But there is more. If you marry and have children several other things are likely to happen. The issue of trust may become even more intense. You may find that your spouse "triggers" outbursts of strong anger or fear that are hard to control, by saying certain words or behaving in a certain way. These triggered outbursts are a sign of PTSD, which we will discuss in detail later.

You may find that you occasionally lose control of your temper with your children, and that it leaves you feeling remorseful and bad about yourself.

You'll Try To Rationalize/Justify

If these things happen, you will probably try to justify them somehow, or you may try to aggressively cow your spouse into going along and agreeing with you. All the while, you will continue to feel bad about yourself underneath, and will be afraid of what these behaviors "mean" about you. It can sometimes be like walking a tightrope, trying to do right while under pressure from the feelings created by your abuse. Pages from my life.

One reason it is hard to be successful with your own family is that you never had a good example from your own parents to follow.

While all this may sound hopeless, it is not! The key to overcoming this kind of bad programming is to first be fully aware of it! What you don't know *can* hurt you! When you realize what you are doing, and why you are doing it, then you can start changing what you don't like. *If you can be programmed to be miserable, you can learn to program yourself to be happier*. It takes hard work, to be sure. But as the Bible says, "The truth will set you free". The truth is not something you should fear, but something you should seek.

More About Love Relationships

Now I'd like to talk more about love relationships.

From all we've covered so far, it should be clear that an abused child will have special needs in the area of love.

First, you will probably need more affection than normal. To be treated with love and affection is a wonderful thing if you have not received enough as a child. It can even be a little overwhelming. When I realized that I shared a true love with the girl who would become my wife, I sobbed uncontrollably for quite a while. To have wanted and needed that for so long, and to finally know it had come was just too much at that moment.

Obviously it helps if the person is gentle, affectionate, accepting and loves you just as you are. It would probably not work for an abuse victim to be with someone who is very selfish, or who is not affectionate. Likewise for someone who is argumentative, critical, disloyal, controlling, or who does not want to understand you. There are big–hearted people out there who will have more than enough love for you. And you will be able to delight in returning that love.

Second, if you have PTSD, you will at times confuse those closest to you with the abusing parent(s). That is hard for loved ones to deal with. For that you need someone who loves you enough to understand you are not meaning to attack them, and who can (try to) tolerate your outbursts and still love and (try to) support you. This is a problem you have to work on together, to minimize the pain for both of you (we'll discuss how later).

Third, you will need to learn to communicate with your special person, even more than average people need to. The better you are at communication, the less pain you will both suffer due to adjusting to the effects of abuse. I will explain how to do this later.

You Are Not A Charity Case

It's important to know that you are not "damaged goods" or a charity case when it comes to love. Love is the special human miracle that brings two people together who find, to their surprise, that they don't want to be apart. And who see and bring out the best in each other.

You don't have to be "cool" or perfect to experience or be worthy of love. It's a miracle that can happen to anyone. Abuse victims can be more loyal, sensitive and giving lovers than average, because they know what it's like to be without it. They are certainly as desirable as anyone else, especially if they have the strength of character to keep trying to heal, to do the right thing, and to not give up.

When looking for a partner, it would be wise to pay attention when you find someone where you both feel very comfortable with each other and both have a feeling that the other person *feels like "home"*. That's the very best sign of all. Superficial things like "coolness" or trophy type looks mean nothing if there is not that mutual comfort. Things like honesty, loyalty, a giving nature and high moral standards are qualities that stand the test of time. Hopefully you will strive to have these qualities, too. Just know that you deserve to have love and happiness in your life as much as the next person. Abuse victims do not lose their capacity to love and be loved.

Now I'll tell you why others may not have noticed your childhood abuse, and failed to help.

Chapter Eight

Appearances Can Be Deceiving

Ask most people who knew me and my family when I was growing up, and they'd probably tell you we were an "ideal family". Abuse? No way! My parents were great people (true), and great parents (hmmm). To all outside appearances, all was well. And that's because the abuse was carefully hidden. I don't think that was planned, but my parents were very smart, and their instincts probably told them to keep it totally private. Even so, at least one relative, when told about the abuse said: "I thought so!" There were a few little clues, and that was it.

I remember one time my mom was on the phone, talking animatedly to a friend, all warm and happy. I tried to ask her an important question, and she suddenly covered the mouthpiece, her happy face turned instantly into her mask of hate, and she snarled at me: "Shut up and leave me alone!" Then she uncovered the mouthpiece, her face instantly transformed back into a smile, and without missing a beat, continued the conversation. I have to admit, that was a little scary, and parallels movie depictions of people possessed by demons. She was adept at showing the outside world the picture she wanted it to see.

And what did that mean about my chances for getting outside help? They were almost nonexistent. I can remember many times praying that someone would see what was happening, and help me. Those prayers were *never* answered. So how many other children like that are there? We can't know, but I'll bet there are plenty.

A Missed Chance For Help

There was only one time I thought I had a chance to get help, and I want to tell you about it.

When I was about 14, things had gotten really bad, and one day I felt I'd taken about as much as I could, announced I was leaving home and stormed out the door. There was a wooded area near our home that I enjoyed hiking in, and a pond where I sometimes skated, often by myself. That day, I headed into the woods, and walked a long time, thinking about my vulnerable position. I knew I'd need an education, and that if I followed through on my threat, I would put myself at a big disadvantage in life. On the other hand, life at home was very painful and difficult. There was constant abuse, harassment, and turmoil.

I had come to the conclusion that I would go back and try harder to tolerate the abuse so I could get an education. Then I would leave home for good, and hopefully never see them again. About that time I saw a patrol car near the pond I frequented, and the policeman motioned me to come over. He asked who I was, then told me my parents had called and asked them to search for me. He then instructed me to get into the patrol car, and he would take me home.

On the way, he began to lecture me about how kids like me don't appreciate their parents enough, and how could I upset them that way, etc., etc. Sitting in the back of the patrol car, I felt really hopeless. That officer didn't care to find out why I had left home, or if I might need his protection. He just didn't care, period. I knew then without a doubt that there would be no one that would ever help me, and I tried to think of the time I could leave home with an education and be left alone to live my life.

Unfortunately, more damage was done after that officer failed to make any effort to at least find out if I needed help or protection. And by the time I did leave home, I was even less able to handle my situation than I might have been had that officer bothered to ask a few questions or listened to what I might have said, and had been able to help.

I'm not angry with the officer—I forgot his name almost immediately. But he turned out to be my only chance, and he was no chance at all.

You May Be Able To Help

People who see the possibility of abuse may be the **only chance** a child has. You do have to be careful about intruding into the privacy of a family, but you can speak with love and concern, and listen to the child. And if there are further signs of abuse, you can use common sense, be there for the child, and try with care and sensitivity to help that child. When the signs are clear, this includes calling the child abuse hotline, where you can be anonymous.

One of the first things I learned as a child welfare social worker is that appearances can be deceiving. What people see, or think they see when looking at a family from the outside can be far from what is really happening. "Ideal" parents sometimes commit terrible crimes upon their children. "Obviously" abusive parents sometimes turn out to be good parents. What the outside world sees can be way off. That's why (ideally) careful investigations are done, and as a result, many families are helped. It is also true that the bureaucracy sometimes makes big mistakes, as we read in the newspaper from time to time. Some workers are very inept, but these are a small minority who are not up to a very tough job, and they don't last long. Most helpers try their best, and some are outstanding.

So if a child complains about their family situation, you can, if there are no signs of immediate danger to the child, just listen, and give your belief and support. They may be able to work it out themselves with your support, or with the help of the school or the clergy. And if they need more, you will hopefully have the courage to help them get it. If you judge the child is in real danger, you must at least call your local abuse hotline, where your identity stays anonymous if you wish.

In these situations, an innocent life may truly be at stake. Now we'll talk about the problem feelings that abuse survivors have.

Part Three

The Problem Feelings
And PTSD

Now we'll look at the difficult feelings that come with abuse: Anger, fear, and grief.

Then we'll talk about the most difficult feelings: PTSD and depression. I'll discuss where I think my feelings came from, and how I gradually learned to handle them.

Chapter Nine

Anger and Grief

When mom abused me, she would be very angry, at times in a rage. And it would come on suddenly, for no apparent reason. Her face was a mask of pure hate. Her teeth would be clenched and showing, her eyes on fire. Often she would hit, usually on the bottom (until I was older), always very hard. This would happen over little things that often didn't make any sense. Naturally, I would feel hurt, scared, outraged and violated, but I didn't dare show these feelings because I felt in real danger.

That happened countless times, and all that outrage I felt had to go somewhere, so it hid inside my head somewhere, without my even knowing it was there. And it came out later in life as occasional excessive anger. I couldn't understand this anger, or why it was there, so I defended by believing it would go away, or that it was somehow justified (when it wasn't). But it kept on popping up, usually to my embarrassment, or shame. I later learned that these "anger incidents" were symptoms of PTSD.

Buried Anger Is A Given

Buried anger, I think, is a certain result of abuse. How could you NOT feel anger, even rage at being violated, and how could you feel safe to show it? So it gets buried, hidden from view. To recover, I think you must connect with that anger, feel its full force, and learn where it comes from. Until you do, when it comes out in a show of vicious temper, or in a rage out of proportion to the situation, you won't know why. You'll just think you have a bad temper, or a tendency to lose control. And you will probably fight to justify it in order to feel comfortable—and you won't be able to. It will be just one more reason to feel bad about yourself.

This anger stays with you until you're able to get in touch with it, remember what happened to cause it, and let it come out in a safe, controlled setting. You must feel its full force in order to understand it and heal it. Of course, this is ONLY safe to do *with a good therapist present* (one of my good ones helped me), and they can help you find the best way to do this.

The Anger Comes From The Past, Not The Present

Once you connect fully with your buried anger, you'll clearly see that it is ONLY appropriate to your abused past. It makes complete sense when you can remember and re-live the actual events that caused you to have and hide this anger. And it makes no sense in the present, where it keeps leaking out. It tends to explode or come out in situations that look or feel "just like" the times you were abused.

The Anger Takes Many Forms

It can be the look on a person's face, or the way they say something. It can morph into "road rage", or other reactions when you feel a little pushed around. It can cause an exaggerated anger reaction in many situations, and can lead you to be abusive yourself at times. These are signs of "triggers", and triggers are indicators of PTSD, which we'll talk about soon.

Learn To Identify Past Anger

Whenever your anger seems out of proportion, or inappropriate to the actual situation, you should suspect it is really the suppressed anger from your *past* leaking out. Of course, when you cool down, you are likely to feel remorseful, if not foolish and embarrassed. Which doesn't help you feel good about yourself. Ironically, this is not your fault, even though you will be held fully responsible for how you behave when the hidden anger does leak out. In this world there are no special exemptions from responsibility. You are being tripped up again by things that were done to you. The good news is that there are ways you can (with help) heal much of this anger.

A Way To Reach The Anger

Here's what I had to do: First, in a therapy setting (the only safe way to do it), I re–lived the events of abuse that created this buried mass of anger. Only then did the anger make sense. Second, I had to fully feel the anger, and feel it directed toward the person(s) who abused me and caused me to feel it. And I had to feel it *as I felt it then*, directed toward the abuser *as they were then*. When you do this, you literally bring the past alive (in a safe setting), and you begin to see why you have the anger.

Healing The Anger

When the anger comes into your conscious mind and is tied to its source, and is felt with full force, that puts it in its proper place, and you are able to heal some of it. It can take a while for all of it to come up, be connected, and be fully felt.

I did this when I was feeling angry for no obvious reason. My therapist asked, "Who are you angry with?" And the images of my parents, at the ages when the abuse happened, came to mind. Then I let myself feel the anger full–force. I bit into a pillow and screamed into it, imagining what I wanted to do to them. Without going into details, the things I wanted to do were quite violent. In fact, I was shocked by that, and by the power of the rage within. And then I felt ashamed of what I had wanted to do. The shame made me realize that this anger had been in me for a long, long time. I couldn't believe it was so strong, so powerful, so raw.

I also made the connection that this was the anger that had been coming out in all sorts of ways, and that it belonged to the past, not the present. Until that moment, I had no idea it was there!

Warning: I'd suggest that if you will be doing this, you wear a "mouthpiece" to protect your teeth. My anger/rage was so strong I cracked a tooth when I did it.

I can't tell you how liberating this was! There was finally a good reason for things that had made no sense to that point. I had to do this a few times to bring it all up, then it ended naturally. The most ironic thing was that my *present* anger toward my parents *decreased* dramatically! Releasing the buried anger made it possible to have a better adult relationship with them, because I was then better able to separate "abused childhood" from the present. As an independent adult, I had nothing more to be angry about, as my parents were behaving much better now.

As I understand it, this hidden anger is *like a boil in your mind*, made of feelings from the past, and once you lance it and release the contents, you heal a lot of it. You may feel it later on, but not as strong, or as often. The one time you will feel it again is when your PTSD is triggered (PTSD involves an automatic reaction to something or someone that feels, sounds or looks like the old abuse). When this happens, you do your best to remember what you've learned, and put the past where it belongs. ***Bringing up hidden anger should be done only with the good helper you have found***. They provide a safe setting, help you interpret your feelings, and help your healing.

Ways To Handle Anger

Since it's likely you've had problems managing anger because of this "hidden rage", let's talk about some well known ways of handling it.

Since we know that some of the anger of an abused person may be out of proportion or inappropriate, there are a few sensible things you can do when you feel angry. First, you can ask yourself *"Who* am I angry with? What am I *really* angry about? Is my anger appropriate to the situation, or does it seem to come from something else? Am I more angry than makes sense, considering the situation?" In my case, while the answers did not all come right away, just thinking about it in a rational way led me to make better decisions about how, or if I would express the anger. Thinking this way gave me more control, and helped me do a better job of handling it.

What Normal Anger Is For

Let's dig deeper into the question of the reasons for anger and expressing it effectively. Anger is a way we draw boundaries around what we consider to be our space, and a way of warning off those who we feel are violating these boundaries. Some common expressions which describe our feelings of violation are: Stepping on toes, being in my space, being too aggressive, being obnoxious, p---ing me off, messing with my head, and so on. In each case we feel violated in some way, and our anger tells the other person to back off.

But abused people have a problem here. They've been so badly violated already that they are much more sensitive to violation, and may even see it when it isn't really there. That's one reason why abused people need to step back from anger and look at the situation rationally.

Assertive vs. Aggressive

One way to handle anger situations is to be *assertive*, instead of being aggressive. Assertiveness is about standing up for yourself in an adult way. Some techniques of assertiveness that I've used are:

- Stating your position politely but firmly, in an objective, non-emotional way

- trying to be as nice as possible–i.e.–assuming the best

- Calmly repeating your position until you are sure you have been fully heard

- If you are getting nowhere, seeking other help if appropriate, repeating the above two steps

- Using the language of whatever you are dealing with. If it's an insurance policy, read it. If a car warranty, use words like "defect" where they apply

- Listen to what the other person is saying, and respond with thoughtful reason

- You can and should modify your request if you think they have a good point

This is a way to stand up for yourself without getting angry.

If The Other Person Is Irrational Or Threatening

You should try to avoid people like this if you have PTSD. They can "trigger"you, and put you in a dangerous or deadly situation (you'll see why soon).

Some things you can do are: Ignore them by not looking at them or responding; go away; refuse to engage. You don't want two out–of–control people.

If someone is being really obnoxious or behaving irrationally, does it make sense to buy into whatever their problem is, or does it make more sense to walk away?

If someone threatens you, does it make sense to threaten them back? Wouldn't walking away make the most sense? Nothing positive can be accomplished in a situation like this.

Try Not To Let The Anger Take Control

As you'll soon see, with PTSD, anger can come suddenly and overwhelm your self–control. People with PTSD must learn to avoid "hot" anger situations, and should avoid escalating or provoking other people who have anger problems. I've had to learn to control these feelings, both during recovery and ongoing.

How I Try To Handle Anger

My own plan is to try to *never* act in anger. As an ideal, I want to be as calm as possible, in full control of myself, and thinking clearly when I try to handle a difficult situation. I'd rather let some time pass than make a fool of myself, and ruin any chance to resolve the problem to my satisfaction. Of course, I can't always do it, but I can try.

That doesn't mean you always have to slink away with your tail between your legs when someone else does something outrageous. There is always the option of deciding whether a response is worth it. Sometimes, after some objective thought, you may decide to put a stop to it, usually by seeking a person in authority (supervisor, manager, police officer, etc.) so you don't have to sit and fume for days afterward.

Stay In Your Adult

The best way to know what is appropriate is to try to get in a rational, adult frame of mind, the best way you can. Then try to make a rational, sensible decision. Have I been triggered into PTSD? Is this a major assault or just a scratch? Does it really matter to me? Should I stand up now, or is it worth the battle? Can I live with just letting go of it and walking away? Should I cool down and let time pass before I act?

I think the best bet for dealing with anger that may be getting out of control is to back off, stop, walk away. Excuse yourself, take a break, take a walk, work it off with exercise. Try to wait until your anger goes away before dealing with the problem, even if it takes a whole day or more. Make it your policy not to act in strong anger. You will think more clearly, and reach a better solution. I can't remember one time that acting in strong anger helped me to solve anything. Sometimes I made a fool of myself. Sometimes I made the situation worse, or said or did things I wanted to take back later. Strong anger rarely helped, and even when it seemed to help, it almost always made me embarrassed.

And you can ask the opinion or help of someone you think is more level–headed.

Are The Experts Right About Triggered Anger?

Anger management experts say that it's not the trigger or action of another that makes us angry, but our *beliefs and attitudes* about those things. I think that PTSD may not work this way. With PTSD, triggers seem to cause an instant, pre-programmed irrational response. *Then* thoughts and beliefs may come into play. That makes things a little more complicated.

Learning To Love Ourselves

Something I've learned recently is that a lot of anger comes from how we see ourselves and others. If we feel unworthy and are insecure, we will take offense more easily. Only when we see that we are completely worthy will we be more secure. Our worthiness should be unconditional, regardless of how anyone treats us. People who were loved as children are likely to feel and know this. Their reaction to angry, disturbed behavior tends to be a mix of puzzlement and sympathy. Abused children don't react this way. But if you think about it, we *are* worthy, and each of us is a miracle. We need to get to the point where we know and believe it.

And if we are worthy, it means everyone is. And if this is so, bad behavior is often the result of ignorance, insecurity or a mistake. Most religions teach this. Jesus' statement, "love your neighbor as yourself" requires that you first love yourself, then you will realize that all others are worthy of love, too. Buddhism teaches this as well (the ideal of loving kindness, which is also to be applied to yourself), and I'm sure you can find it in all religions.

All I know is that it's a good attitude to have. More good things happen when you approach life this way.

Ways To Learn More

There are some other things that tap into this way of looking at life, and I've begun to look into them recently. One *really* good one is **mindfulness meditation**. Mindfulness is a discipline that brings your mind into the present moment (you'd be surprised at how rarely you are there). And some people find help from Tai Chi, yoga, and other disciplines. I'd recommend you explore these and related subjects to see if they can help you find more peace.

As a recent trip to a bookstore showed, there are many books about anger and anger management. You can browse through them and see if any seem to give good sensible advice. As always, I recommend reading promising books to broaden your outlook and to find useful ideas. That's what I did over the years.

For mindfulness I recommend anything by Dr. Jon Kabat–Zinn. Dr. Kabat–Zinn is excellent at interpreting Eastern methods for western people.

What I'm saying is, you'll probably need to learn new attitudes and beliefs about anger if you have been abused and suffer from PTSD and/or depression. We survivors of child abuse are bound to have problems with anger because of what happened to us, and we can learn to handle it! We should use all the resources available to us to learn, including a therapist.

If you have a well of buried anger from abuse, you can heal a lot of it. Once you do, you'll find that anger is not the problem it once was. You can then learn and practice rational, adult ways of handling the normal scrapes and bumps of life.

Grief

PTSD from child abuse is caused by trauma that can begin at birth and continue throughout childhood. That's a lot of trauma. You can get PTSD from a single incident. But *what if trauma is a way of life*?

How can a child grow and develop normally when they're constantly abused? How can they learn trust when a parent can't be trusted? Or learn to love themselves when a parent tears them down daily? For an abused child, their emotional foundation is very shaky. They just don't get the love and nurturing needed to grow into a strong and happy adult.

This leads to more anxiety, more stress, more depression, and more problems than a person raised with love will have.

You Have Suffered A Great Loss

Since you "only go around once" in life, you can't ever get back what you have lost. While you can learn to fully love your spouse and children, and can receive and enjoy their love, you can't ever regain the love you needed—and lost—as a child.

That is a *tremendous* loss to suffer! And like all other major losses, it must be grieved before you can let go of it and go on with your life. My experience is that any time I have a major loss (death, etc.), my grief seems to be magnified by the loss due to the abuse.

What You Can Do

What can we do about this? First, we can be honest about our feelings, and let ourselves feel our grief for a *reasonable, limited* time. Because of the childhood losses, we can sometimes get stuck in grief, and if this happens we can seek the help of our good therapist. "Over–grieving" can bring on depression, which will not help at all. We have to limit how much we feel at a given time, and not overwhelm ourselves. One way is to combine grieving with some fun activity–take a break.

Another technique for controlling this is what a therapist called the left arm/right arm method: First, touch your left arm, and let yourself feel the grief, however deep it goes. Then, touch your right arm and think of all the good things in your life, and some of the best moments you have had. In this way you can learn to take a break from bad feelings when you want or need to.

Grief is a normal process that we must go through when we suffer a big loss. People with PTSD due to child abuse have a special kind of loss to grieve, and it's just something you will have to do. Remember that the purpose of grieving is to be able to let go of the past and move forward.

A Time To Grieve And A Time To Let Go

Once you've let yourself grieve, then it's time to say: "The past is over, and it's time to begin looking toward a better future. I accept what I've lost, because that was out of my hands. Now I can influence what the rest of my life will be."

I *strongly* recommend you get help with grief, because it can spark depression if overdone. If you feel this happening, get the help you need to get unstuck and to move on. If you get stuck like this, try counting your blessings—all the good things in your life—and keep them in the front of your mind. I've found that mindfulness meditation helps at these times.

People with PTSD especially need to learn how to count their blessings, and go forward toward the good things of life.

Now we'll talk about another difficult emotion–fear.

Chapter Ten

Dealing With Your Fears

Have you ever seen a dog that's been badly abused? The fear such an animal shows toward human contact is heartbreaking. We adopted a dog like that once, a collie we named Betty. I had to carry her home in my arms, because she was too frozen with fear to walk. Well, Betty warmed up over the time we had her, and enjoyed life just fine, but she always stayed shy.

Abuse Creates Fears

People aren't much different. Being abused creates fears. The fears will depend on what kind of abuse actually happened. And sometimes fear can be strong enough to cause PTSD, which we'll discuss in the next chapter. For people *without* serious problems, it can work to deny fear. For abuse victims, it can't. Abuse can cause crippling fears, just like it can cause irrational anger. And like with anger, if you try to deny, it will only get you into deeper trouble.

Fears Are Very Hard To Admit—For A Reason

Many people act like they would rather die than admit to a weakness or a problem. This is something that comes from our life experience. We must be tough to survive. We all know this is true, and are taught it both by parents and authority figures, and by the reality of the street growing up. Showing weakness or fear brings bad consequences.

This creates a big problem for the abused, who must deal with their fears in order to recover. That's because the fears of an abused person are so much stronger and more crippling than average. The whole world tells you not to admit to fear, but you have to do just that to recover! Thanks a lot, world.

What Is Real Strength?

If real strength is standing up to fear, then the fear you must first stand up to is the fear of being afraid, or somehow weak. So being *truly* strong is having the guts to admit to and face your fears, not running and hiding from them! Being strong is not giving up until you have conquered your fears. Being strong is doing what's right for yourself and your loved ones no matter what anybody thinks. That's *real* strength.

The overwhelming fears you have are set in the help-lessness and dependency of early childhood. People who haven't had this happen to them will not easily understand. They will show disapproval, and expect you to act macho or fearless, like they do. This can put you in a bind, because disapproval is hard on an abused person. And denying your fears will keep you trapped in them. It can even be a suicidal trap.

In order to recover from your fears, you'll not only need the courage to stare them right in the eye until you know the whole truth about them. You'll also need the courage to endure the occasional disapproval of others as you tackle your problems. This takes much more courage and character than those who disapprove are ever likely to be called on to show. You can be proud of yourself when you *do* face these things.

Where They Come From

Let's review some of my fears and their origins:

- Fear of *abandonment*, because you were either threatened with it or you were actually abandoned by one or both parents

- Fear of *being defective, no good, worthless*, because that's what you were always told by your parent(s)

- Fear of *being unlovable*, because your parent(s) did not give you love

- Fear of *self–assertion/being yourself*, because you were punished and abused for doing so

- Fear of *standing up for yourself*, because you were viciously punished if you did

- Fear of *losing control*, because you could never control what happened to you

- Fear of *admitting you have a problem*, because it would mean you really are defective

- *Paranoia*, because your parent(s) really was out to get you

- Fear of *making a mistake*, because you were severely punished or abused when you did

- Fear of *something really bad about to happen*, especially if you are happy, because that's how the abuse came

- Fear of *getting a terminal illness*, because you believe you are defective and your luck is bad (or hypochondria, which is a way your fears attach to your body, so they appear to have a physical basis)

- Fear of *premature death*, mixed with other fears, because you were told you would be put to death for your "transgressions"

- Fear of *an intimate relationship*, especially if the abuser was the opposite sex, because you will feel the opposite sex is abusive and controlling. And because your partner will find out you are defective, unlovable, etc., and/or they will abandon you, just like mom or dad did

This list does not include all the fears you may have. There are plenty of other possibilities. One thing that should be clear about these fears is that ***they have a basis in reality***. They did not come out of thin air, or appear because you are "too sensitive". These fears were taught to you. Maybe even pounded into you. They are real fears, caused by things that really happened (even though they are not appropriate now). It's very important for you to see that. Yes, they cause you problems, and probably have no basis in *present* reality. But that's not your fault. You came by them honestly.

What You Can Do

Now for the big question: What can you do about it?

Let's suppose you've decided to face your fears and learn how to handle or get over them. And you understand that the fears are legitimate because what made you afraid was real in your abusive childhood. And you realize the fears you have today come from that childhood experience, and that you still have them because that's just how our minds work—it's human nature. And you agree that it's better to fix the fears than to go on beating yourself because you have them. Here's how I did it:

The first lesson is: ***"That was then, this is now"***. From now on, when you are afraid, think: "Is this fear from then, or is it from now?" Sure, something in the present triggered it (a thought, a memory, an event, etc.), but the important question is: "Is it based on abuse in the past, or is it based purely on the present?" This is important, because the first thing you have to learn is to ***separate the past from the present***. One reason you're unhappy is that your present is being held hostage by your past. In the real present, you have great opportunity for happiness and enjoyment of life. So you might say that your job is to *cut*

as much of your hurtful past out of the present as possible.
And to learn how to do this, you have to first separate past
from present.

Practice, Practice, Practice

This takes practice. When a fear comes up, ask "what
am I really afraid of?" Keep asking until you're sure you
have the right answer. Don't worry if it takes hours or days
or even weeks to figure one out. It *will* come to you. It
would help to write the fears down. Work on filling out
your list of fears that come from abuse, and note the actual
event(s) that created each one. Yours will probably look
something like my list, above.

Make the effort to connect these fears to the actual
events that created them, so you can really understand why
you have them. Then, whenever a fear comes up that you
have already surveyed, remember where it came from and
why you have it. The more aware you are in your conscious mind, the less grip a given fear will have, and the
less fearful you will be in general. Fears like these tend
to reinforce each other, so **when you diminish one you
diminish all**, which builds happiness.

A Time To Use Help

If you choose to do this, I advise you to receive help
from your good helper, because the feelings attached to the
abuse events are very strong (strong enough to make you
afraid all your life). The helper can also help you make
connections that will save you time and unnecessary pain.

When You're Ready, Share A Fear

It can help with abuse-created fears to admit and talk about them with those closest to you. After much aggravation over the years, I realized and admitted to my wife that I feared she would abandon me. I had interpreted some of her behavior to "mean" that this could happen. When I told her, she couldn't understand where it came from, and thought it was ridiculous. The idea had never crossed her mind. She assured me that this was not going to happen, which in turn helped me to be less afraid.

When you have fears like this, you can see things that aren't there. These fears and your interpretations of others' behavior are coming from what happened to you when you were abused, just like when the abused dog cringes if you innocently raise your hand. There's nothing crazy or weird about this. It's how you've reacted to being abused, as anyone would have.

By talking these feelings over with an accepting person, and helping both yourself and those close to you understand them, you can improve your relationships and your own outlook. This can lead to recovery and better times.

Anxiety

Anxiety is a state of being that is related to fear. An excess of fear can lead to a state of anxiety. The anxiety can then take on a life of its own, and can dominate your life. Long lasting anxiety can breed or be a part of many different anxiety disorders (acute anxiety, PTSD, panic, etc.).

The Physical Part

Anxiety has a strong physical part. During anxiety, the body may produce high levels of stress hormones, such as cortisol. It may also produce high levels of adrenaline. These and other substances can stress the body in many ways, causing eventual health problems. Often it is necessary to find a way to reduce anxiety to free up energy for recovery, and to protect your health. Medications may be prescribed for this. Besides SSRI anti–depressants, some popular ones have been xanax, klonopin, and other anti–anxiety and tranquilizer medications (**note warnings about these to come**). Recently, propranolol has been used more than before for anxiety and PTSD. We'll talk about all these in more detail soon.

Cut Out Caffeine

One big help for people suffering from anxiety is simple: Cut out stimulants such as caffeine. I did this with very good results.

Practice Stress Reduction

There are many ways to reduce anxiety besides medication. One or more of the following may help: Exercise (walking, running, weight training, housework, gardening, etc. I've found this to help a lot). Yoga (stretching postures, often combined with meditation. This helps, especially when you get older). Meditation, especially mindfulness (I'll talk more about this later. I've found it to help a lot).

More On Medications

First, ***anything I tell you about medications in this book are my opinions, not medical advice. I give them both to tell of my own experience, and to help you think clearly about your own. You must have a physician to receive medications, and I recommend you find one who is willing to answer all your questions about them, and help you decide what is right for you.***

Let's note here that medications can sometimes help a great deal. There are many disorders besides PTSD or depression that can be present. Panic disorder, obsessive–compulsive disorder, and manic–depressive disorder can all be factors, depending on your brain chemistry. Or, you could have one or more of these things as personality traits (means they are there but mild and under your control).

There are many different medications now that can reduce fear, anxiety and worry, leaving you with the energy you need to make good progress. They can also make you more comfortable. Many *anti–depressants* now are pretty safe and effective for most people. But some drugs really don't work that well for some people. This is what a good doctor is for. It's worth the effort to find one who will help but not over–medicate.

Be warned: A member of my family was nearly killed by an incompetent psychiatrist prescribing inappropriate medications, and with inappropriate dosages and combinations. Always research medications before taking or changing them, and ask a trusted doctor or pharmacist if you have questions!

Side effects, when present, can sometimes be reduced by using smaller doses (under supervision). Most anti–depressants work by allowing more "good feelings" chemicals to build up in your brain. This can make you feel in a better mood, and can also make your mood more steady and calm. We'll talk more about medications in chapter 12.

Warning

I would be careful with tranquilizers, and even some anti-anxiety meds. Some of them can be addictive, or can cause such bad withdrawal symptoms that some people can't get off of them. They should be used with extra care for that reason *(something to ask your doctor about)*. That said, sometimes it's better to take what you're told than resist. It may be a matter of how much pain you're in, and how well you can function.

I've had good luck with *propranolol* for anxiety. It blocks formation of adrenaline in the body. **But** there can be dangers for the heart in some people with this medication, and it should only be taken under supervision of a physician, if they feel it may help you.

Many people have a fear of medications, thinking that taking it means you're weak, or the medicine will somehow change you into another person. Neither is true. All they really may do, when used under supervision, is help you get better and enjoy life more (*but be careful*). A couple of medications have made a big difference for me. I'll talk more about my experiences with medications in chapter 12.

The Best Is Medication and Talking Therapy

Science tells us that the best results come from a combination of medication and talking therapy. The most successful type of talking therapy reported so far is cognitive behavioral therapy, which we've already gone over. I'll talk more about this in a later chapter.

In this therapy you do assignments to help you learn to be more in the reality of the present moment. Note that this is also the goal of mindfulness, which has helped me in exactly this way . We'll talk more about this, too.

Now let's take a look at PTSD. What is it? How does it work? What can you do if you have it?

Chapter Eleven

All About PTSD

The Puzzle

The man and his wife were arguing about some little thing. They were both tired, and the argument was escalating. Then, something she said infuriated him. He suddenly began to shout, as though consumed with rage. He felt attacked and betrayed, and was losing control of his anger.

He kept yelling, and she yelled back, and then he grabbed a rattan stack table and began to bang it on the floor, until it came apart. When it was completely shattered, he realized he was getting out of control, and he abruptly stalked out of the room, slamming the door behind him.

Alone, he began to cry softly. His feelings were coming in overwhelming waves: Anger, fear, hurt, betrayal, abandonment. Depression was setting in quickly. She was in tears, feeling like she had committed some terrible sin, and angry because of the seeming unfairness of it all.

Welcome to the wonderful world of "Complex" PTSD!

This had happened many times before, and they were both still baffled by it. What was wrong? Why did he feel that way. How could they stop it from happening again? For a long time we couldn't find the answers.

But after over 30 years of struggling blindly along, I was seeing a therapist briefly (a good one), when she said: "Sounds like you may have PTSD". "PTS what?" I said. "Here", she said, "Take these books home and see what you think". And sure enough, there I was on the pages of those books! Suddenly, it all became clear, and everything finally made sense. Now I knew why I had behaved and felt as I had for all my life. And somehow I knew that getting past it would not be as hard as it had been to understand it.

What Is PTSD?

According to Webster's, PTSD is "a psychological reaction after experiencing a highly stressing event, usually characterized by depression, anxiety, flashbacks, recurrent nightmares, and avoidance of reminders of the event".

Other sources say that *"complex"* PTSD results from *repeated* trauma that happens over a long period of time, and that *sexual, physical and emotional child abuse* are a cause of this kind. I think it's called "complex" because it happens while a child is developing into an adult, and the abuse hinders normal development, which in turn can cause a whole lot of other problems. The problems it causes depend on what actually happens to the child, and when. And it also depends on the child's emotional makeup.

You might guess there can be different problems of different degrees, depending on what actually happened to any person, and this is true. *So it's not "one size fits all"*. That's why I've said from the beginning that our PTSD reactions will be different. And I've also said and believe that there are many things common to most if not all sufferers of PTSD.

Depression and PTSD

The experts also say that depression and PTSD go hand in hand, and a standard treatment for PTSD is SSRI anti–depressants. In my case, whenever a PTSD reaction was triggered, the immediate emotional storm of anger, anxiety, fear, etc. was usually followed quickly by severe depression.

In fact, until I was told about PTSD, I always thought my problem was depression.

Some More Facts and Thoughts About PTSD

So PTSD, or Post Traumatic Stress Disorder is something that can happen if you were abused as a child. It doesn't always happen, but often does. You may have heard of it being associated with combat, and in WW–I it was called "shell shock". The diagnosis of PTSD did not exist until 1980. One main feature of PTSD is a perceived or real threat of being killed, or actually seeing someone die. This can include a feeling of complete helplessness and the belief and/or feeling that death is imminent. It's clear to see how this can happen in battle.

And if you are a small child being constantly and severely threatened, you are at least as helpless and vulnerable, probably more so. In either case, you feel trapped, with no way out. In fact, I've had doctors tell me that PTSD/child abuse can be the hardest kind of all to recover from (not that any kind is easy), because you are never as helpless as when you're very young. And because it happens when you are developing as a person. It was hard, all right, but I have gotten better. That's why I think others can too.

Growing Up Into PTSD

Let's look at what it's like for the abused child. Imagine a baby, toddler or small child being abused and threatened by an out–of–control parent, who is screaming, perhaps hitting, or even worse. Can that child stand up and defend itself? How do they deal mentally with being hurt, despised and badly used by the one(s) they must depend on for love, nurturing and care? What do they do with the anger they feel? Is it realistic to fear being killed, especially if the abuse escalates, or the parent repeatedly says "I will kill you"? (Never mind small child. As a teenager, I remember locking my bedroom door at night after a friend of mine was murdered by his mother). What kind of control does a child have if a parent chooses to control them through terror? Or if they just appoint them designated punching bag? Absolutely none.

The Birth Of PTSD

So, what happens to your young mind in this situation? Many things. Feelings shut down, because they are too overwhelming (and, in the case of anger, life threatening). And somehow, over time, the overwhelming fear and panic you feel is burned into a part of your brain as a "feeling memory", and is forevermore associated with the things the abusing parent is saying and doing to you. And in the future, when someone (a spouse, child, boss, authority figure, or even a stranger) seems to behave *just like* the abusing parent, or says the same things, or even looks at you the same way, you can be *triggered* into PTSD.

What It Can Feel Like

When later in life, you are triggered in one of these ways, you are ***instantly*** flooded with those feelings you had at the time of the abuse, and you will feel and believe it is happening again. In *feelings* and *belief*, you are *in the reality* of your former abuse. This is instantaneous, and is not preceded by thought, only by a trigger. Some psychologists label these states hallucinations, or in the extreme, psychosis. I suppose in some people it could reach that point from time to time, but my experience is that these states are more like delusions, which pass in a relatively short time.

By that I don't mean to minimize the intensity, severity or pain of these states. For example, I'm pretty sure I had two bouts of catatonia 35 years ago, which is a psychotic state where you are paralyzed and can't speak. Each time

I had to fight my way out of it, which took a while. It was scary, but it never happened again. I think this just showed how deep this complex PTSD can go. So if you sometimes have had some odd, scary things going on in your head, know that it may have been part of your PTSD, and that it happened because you didn't know about the PTSD yet. Or you may have other disorders in varying degrees as well. If these things keep happening, you should share them with your good therapist. In my experience, when the PTSD eased up, other issues also eased up.

What Are Triggers?

I'd say a trigger is a person or situation, or something coming from that person or situation that *feels just like* when you were being abused as a child. It causes an instant reaction in you of some mix of anger or rage, fear or panic. At this time it is as though you have been instantly transported back to an incident of past abuse, and it is real in your feelings and in your mind.

Before I knew it was PTSD, I usually believed it was real. But that never made sense, so I just wound up confused and scared by it.

What Triggers Look And Feel Like

What I'm about to tell you is only to help you understand the feeling and experiencing of triggers. While there is *no scientific basis* for there being different types of triggers, I noticed I had different feelings and reactions to different triggering events. Breaking them down as "fear–based" or "anger–based" helped me understand them better. I also think fear and anger are sometimes combined.

Anger Based Triggers

With anger–based triggers, the trigger for me is a person ***acting like*** the abusing parent somehow. Then I instantly react, not merely with anger, but with anger multiplied many times, or *rage*. Certainly there are feelings of both fear and anger, but anger seems to dominate, and I react with instant rage, which I must try to control (the more abusive the triggering person is, the more fear there will also be).

Fear Based Triggers

With fear–based triggers, it's more of a panicky reaction to a ***situation that once brought on abuse***. It is more about loss of control. In my case, the triggered fear is that I will fail to do something I'm expected to do. Or that something is going terribly wrong. The outcome does not appear to be under my control. There is a strong feeling that I am going to die because I will disappoint someone, or fail badly, or that I'll be overwhelmed. This is how I felt when I was being abused—that I would die (or be abandoned) if I didn't do the impossible, or did something wrong, or disappointed the abusing parent. And with fear–based triggers, I instantly react, not with fear, but with fear multiplied many times, or *panic*.

Or, again, a trigger could be a mixture of anger and fear, or action plus situation. That is, loss of control and rage at the same time.

The first time I remember the fear kind happening was when I was 5 years old. I'd been walked to kindergarten by an older child, and it was raining. Somehow, the costume I was carrying under my raincoat for a school party slipped away and was lost. I found out after my escort had left me in front of the school, and panicked. I ran home, right in front of several cars, whose blaring horns only made me panic more. Luckily, I made it home in one piece, and sobbed for hours afterward. My mom didn't kill me for losing the costume, as expected. She just seemed puzzled as to why I had panicked like that.

In anger–based triggers, it is as though the ***person*** who is there now has been transformed into the abusing parent. And you feel that you are re–living the abuse. You feel the same anger (maybe with a little fear), and possibly depression you felt then. When this happens, you may be filled with anger and other emotions, and may have trouble controlling yourself. These emotions are *very* strong. You may lash out, or strongly want to. You may quickly plunge into deep depression. Or you may have other bad reactions. You are in a flood of emotional pain. It's a hell on earth, and it happens every time you are triggered in this way.

In fear–based triggers, it's a seemingly impossible ***situation*** that brings back the past reality. You feel you will fail or have failed, and because of this you will die or be abandoned. This is related to a real demand that has been made of you in the present. You may have trouble with this on a new job, or in any situation where you have little confidence in your ability to perform, or which you fear you can't control, but "have to". You are flooded with feelings of panic, hopelessness, and inadequacy. This makes it hard to do new or unfamiliar things. Anything new or different can be scary and threatening. There can be frustration which turns to anger, which can turn inward, and fuel feelings of self–hate. This can bring on suicidal urges, and/or deep depression. A slightly different form of the same hell on earth.

PTSD As a "Reality Disorder"

PTSD is considered by experts to be an anxiety disorder, and there is certainly plenty of anxiety with it. I think of it more as a reality disorder, because the underlying problem for me has always been the conflict between the reality of the present, and the reality of triggered "feeling memories" of the abuse I suffered.

You Can't Just Ignore It

When you are *not* being triggered, you can be normal in every way. And the feeling of being in another, past reality is temporary, and passes. You are not warped or crazy, and you are capable of the same happiness, love and success as anyone else. But if you are triggered often enough, you can be handicapped by the disorder (if the triggering person or situation remains present). It is likely to be a handicap, because you have no idea where these feelings are coming from, so you don't know how to handle or control them.

And it's likely to get worse over time. You can find yourself living perpetually in survival mode, just getting through day after day, as I did for so many years, and missing a lot from life. Also, repeated episodes erode your morale and self–image, and set the stage for deepening, severe depression. So it's vital to come to grips with PTSD if you have it.

Fortunately, handling PTSD is something I have continued to get better at, considering the pain and disruption of life that it caused me for so many years.

As usual, I am recommending you handle PTSD with the help of a good therapist who specializes in PTSD. There are strong feelings involved, and a well-trained therapist will know the right approach and pace for you. Using a therapist is not only safer, but can save *years* of unnecessary pain and suffering. It only makes sense to have one. And it's worth the trouble to find the right one for you.

What You Can Do About It

Knowing What's Going On Helps

First, just ***knowing*** you have PTSD and how it works can cause everything to suddenly make sense. That's how it was for me. When you are triggered, you are suddenly living in your abusive past *in your feelings.* How you feel and behave *doesn't make much sense in the present*, to you or to those around you. You can feel and appear to act "crazy".

This in turn will cause you to either feel bad about

yourself (which further reinforces the negative self–image caused by the past abuse), or to defend yourself by rationalizing that your feelings are appropriate to the present, which they are not. In so rationalizing, you are likely to be abusive toward whoever triggered the PTSD. And you may both feel bad and defend at the same time.

It's not hard to see how, if it keeps happening, you may spiral down into deep depression, and your self–image may become more and more negative. Also, the people around you will be confused by your behavior, and this will cause relationship problems.

Not a pretty picture. ***It's only when you know where these feelings are coming from, and why you are feeling them that you can start learning to control them.***

Learning What Your Triggers Are

The second thing you need to do is to learn to ***be aware*** of when you have been triggered, and are in PTSD. This is not as easy as it sounds, but can be done with practice. Think about it. When you are triggered, you are suddenly in a *past reality.* It feels true, and you believe it, but it's not real now. The feelings are real, but it's just an echo from your past, let loose by an association (words, attitudes, tone of voice, perception of failure, etc) with that past. That association is the link between now and then. The feelings are real, but you are being fooled by the disorder. You are *not* being abused now, but have merely been *reminded* of the abuse, in living color and surround sound.

That means *you can learn to ignore or "discount" these feelings*, and to see them for what they are. The person or situation that triggers you is *not* responsible for your feelings, so their temporary association in your mind as an abuser or "failure situation" is *false*. The person or situation has nothing to do with it. The wrong button has simply been pressed, either by an unsuspecting person or by a situation you are in.

To recover from PTSD, you have to get these things straight in your mind, and change your perception of what is happening. It's something that was done to you, and is nothing to be ashamed of. At first, it's not easy to tell you are in PTSD, because it feels real. *But once you've learned about how it works in your case, it will dawn on you at some point: " Hey, I think this may be my PTSD, because it doesn't make sense." This happens in your rational mind, not your feelings.*

A Turning Point

The first time this happens can be a turning point in your ability to control the problem. It is cause for celebration! In that moment of recognition, your recovery leaps forward. Then you practice recognizing your PTSD. Soon you will have a list of people and things they say or do that trigger you. After a while, you will find yourself thinking: "Hey, this is my PTSD" more and more often, and sooner and sooner in the cycle. You have to learn how to do this, because the technique I will now describe depends on your recognizing your PTSD happening *as soon as possible.*

Speed Matters!

The technique is simply this: ***As fast as you can***, you must try to shut the past reality down. You say to yourself: "This is my PTSD. This is not real. It is a residue of my past abuse, and has nothing to do with the present. I have just become conditioned to react this way, and I can choose to ignore it. I can choose the present over the past". You can say whatever works for you, but the key is to shut it down as fast as possible. The hard part is that you have to do this when you are experiencing an overwhelming crap–storm of emotions. So when you've succeeded, you can give yourself a high-five.

You need to be fast because the longer you are in PTSD, the harder it is to shut down, and the longer it will take to settle down afterward. And you also want to short circuit the depression that may quickly follow. PTSD is like an emotional earthquake. When it's over, the ground seems shaky for a while. You don't feel safe or secure for a while. ***For some reason, the longer it goes on, the worse it gets***. So the instant you recognize it, no matter how bad you feel, or how upset and in pain you are, ***you must take action to shut it down right away***. The sooner you can do it, the easier it will be on you, and on those around you.

Stop Pouring Gasoline On The Fire

After you are able to keep new fuel from being poured on the fire, the feelings will continue to hurt for a while, but if you are patient, they will fade away. ***It helps to be good to yourself when coming down from PTSD***. Give yourself a treat or distract yourself with one of your favorite activities.

If the person who triggered you is your spouse, they can help in a big way.

What The Spouse Or Friend Can Do

Reacting as quickly as possible is very important. The sooner you can recognize PTSD and start helping, the less pain there will be all around. One of the hardest things to get past may be how you see what is happening. Suddenly, the sufferer may become extremely angry or emotional over some small thing. Since you have not experienced child abuse, and do not understand this behavior, *you will likely become angry or frustrated or defensive yourself.* If the sufferer is appearing to be abusive, you will feel hurt, angry, etc. Then you may escalate the situation and make the PTSD worse.

Make no mistake. This is a normal reaction. The PTSD is *not* your fault, and you have not committed a cardinal sin. You just accidentally pushed their button, and it is one heck of a button! But just as you didn't mean to set the PTSD off, you surely don't want to make it worse. Because you don't want to suffer, and because you love the sufferer, and want to help them if you can. And you don't want to pour gasoline on the fire either.

Since the behavior is not something you understand, you may also measure it against "normal", and decide they are faking, exaggerating, manipulating, or trying to hurt you for no apparent reason. *None of these things is true.*

They are involuntarily experiencing their past abuse. They are in excruciating emotional pain, and are having a lot of trouble controlling floods of emotion, including anger, fear and panic. They are not doing it to hurt you. They are fighting for control of their disorder, and may not always be winning. At that moment, they may be feeling that you are their (past) abuser, because some innocent thing you said or did triggered an association that set it in motion.

Important: If you find that you always react to the PTSD with hurt or strong anger, even though you know the PTSD is not your fault, you'll want to understand why you react that way, and that your feelings are important. Especially if you feel like you're being accused of something when it happens. You need to understand why you feel that way.

You won't be able to help much if you don't take the time to learn why you feel this way, and your reaction can make things worse for both of you. You need to know and remember that *your feelings are just as important* as the one with the PTSD (we'll cover this more in the relationships section).

Very Important: It is normal that the sufferer's pain may soon cause you to also feel overwhelming pain. If you can, try to push through your pain and stay sympathetic. The PTSD sufferer is much less able to do this because they are not completely "there". If you can't hang on, it will be the blind leading the blind. Just try to be kind, and see if you can find a helper good at both PTSD and family therapy.

Some Signs Of PTSD

If you can see what's really going on, and know that it's not your fault, you can be the sufferer's best friend, when they need you the most. You can help them shut the PTSD down. Here's how:

First, recognize the signs of PTSD. Some of these are:

- Overreacting to a small thing. Making a mountain out of a molehill.

- Strong, sudden anger or upset when it doesn't seem appropriate.

- The face turning into a mask of hate or anger.

- Sudden violence, like banging on a table. Loud yelling or ranting.

When you see a sign, resist taking it personally. This is the residue of unbearable pain for what happened to them in their home as a child. It seems directed at you, but it is not. It is really being directed at the abuser, for whom you are standing in (my wife has sometimes said: "Thanks, mom"). Your loved one is in a far away and very bad reality right now, and wants badly to get out of it.

Things That Helped Us

First, if you can't do the things that worked for me and my wife, that's O.K. Just get help from a family/PTSD therapist. to do these things.

Here's what we worked out:

Try not to get caught up in something you're really not a part of. Learn to resist getting angry as much as you can, and take some of the following healing actions, *if and when you are able*:

Speak to the abused child. Apologize, saying, "I'm sorry I hurt you. I would never hurt you on purpose. You are a good person, and you don't deserve to be in pain. You deserve to be loved, and I love you." *The most important thing to say is, "I promise I'll be careful not to say/do that again"*. That's because at this time the sufferer feels that you are in control of their happiness. They know that by saying or doing certain things, you can make them suffer. So they need to hear that you will not knowingly do that to them while they are in PTSD. When not in PTSD, they do know it.

Afterward, the sufferer will be shaken up to some degree, may be depressed, and may be very remorseful (once they are back in present reality). There are two things you can do to help then. First, be careful not to foster guilt, which could start it up again, or deepen the depression (no gas on the coals). Say, "I know you didn't mean what you did/said. You were in terrible pain and couldn't help it for a while. It's O.K.". You are then likely to get profuse apology.

Another thing that can help, if you're up to it, is to give the person a massage, including the feet. This seems to release "good" chemicals. Being kind and loving is the way to go, which is a good policy in any case, if you think about it. And you should be getting the same when there is no PTSD.

Finally, keep saying and doing these things until the sufferer can hear you. Depending on the severity of the attack, this can take some time. Patience helps. Realize that the sufferer may already be in a deep depression, and will need time and kindness until he can pull himself back together, and feel some solid ground under his feet. You can suggest a pleasant activity. Don't try to take over, or overreact out of guilt (which is also false). The sufferer has to take care of himself. Avoid whatever triggers you know about, and do the best you can to allow space for recovery– to–normal. It's still not your fault, and if you make a mistake, keep trying, gently and patiently. *Ultimately, it's the sufferer who has to take control and right his boat. You can only be a helper.*

Your Feelings Count Too

If you feel great pain in these situations, try telling the sufferer in a kind way and at a time when they are normal and strong (not now). Let them know you will not stop trying to help, and that you love them enough to endure pain for them. Don't foster guilt, just be kind. This may help the sufferer learn more about trying to handle the PTSD. They should care about your feelings when they are not in PTSD. This is all part of learning to work as a team.

Becoming A Team

Over time, as you both learn how to control the PTSD, you can become an effective team for recovery. It gets easier and easier to handle, to the point where it becomes, believe it or not, a *small* problem! That's how it worked for me and my wife. It wasn't easy, but we both kept trying and eventually succeeded.

What About The Children?

Things get more complicated if children are present. Unfortunately, children can sometimes trigger PTSD. You've heard that child abuse is a generation–to–generation problem, and that's one way it happens.

With PTSD, the sufferer can wind up being abusive to their own child, no matter how much they've vowed not to, because in PTSD the sufferer is not in complete control, and is in a past reality. Also, deep depression and talk of suicide are very hard for a child to handle.

This is an awful thing to happen, and the *best* reason to work hard on your healing and recovery. If you are abusive to your own child, you are justified in feeling guilt about doing so, no matter what the reason. No parent is excused from the responsibilities of protecting and nurturing their child. You and your spouse must do whatever is necessary to see that your child is loved, nurtured and protected.

The good news is that, as you recover, you can be the good parent you want to be.

We'll talk a lot more about how you can break the chain of abuse and be a good parent in chapter 20, when we look closer at our important relationships. For now, just know that you *can* be a good parent, and that the best thing you can do for your child is to recover.

Problems At Work

Avoiding Treatment

For those with PTSD there can be special problems at the workplace. First, because having a mental disorder carries a stigma in the real world, you will likely hide your problem to protect yourself and your job (a realistic fear). This may cause you to avoid treatment, and that will make your situation worse. You'll have to find a way around that and get the help (and medication) you need.

You Need A Good Boss

Second, your boss or supervisor is a potential trigger for PTSD. If the person over you is sadistic or even just harsh or abusive, you will likely try to stifle the feelings these people arouse. ***This will not work for you.*** If you are in such a situation, you need to plan to make a change. If you don't plan and move in this direction, you are likely to quit without something else to go to, when it becomes intolerable. And that *will* happen if you don't plan and take control of the situation. You may become a job–hopper. You may confuse the intolerable personal situation with the job itself, and conclude you don't like that kind of job, when the real problem is a person who keeps triggering you.

The problem here is that anyone who stands in for the abusing parent can trigger you. It may be people of only one sex, or it may be of both. While you can work this out with a husband or wife, you can't do much about it at work, except get a different job. Whenever you look for a job, ***pay attention to the people you will work for***. This can be the *most* important factor for you. Avoid a workplace where your potential boss gives you a bad vibe, and give extra weight where you feel a good one.

That said, you can't always avoid pain in the working world. It's that way for everybody. Sometimes you may have to look ahead, make plans, and tolerate a bad situation for a little while until the plans work out.

How To Handle The Unfamiliar

Also, on new jobs, or in unfamiliar situations, you may get panicky because you fear change. When this happens, I've found that the best thing to do is to try to break the problem down into manageable pieces. Get information about what is unknown or unclear. Then work on the *parts* of the problem you do understand. This will usually bring more useful information to light, or will make obvious what you need to find out next.

Keep pecking away at it, and you'll soon find the problem is solved. And just accept your feelings. You're not a wimpy bungler, you've just been trained, under threat of death, to *feel* the situation is impossible. You can learn how to control these feelings, and do the things you are afraid to do. Be proud when you are able to do this—it's not easy, but it is doable. Once you get past it, your confidence will grow.

Triggers Make Bad Decisions

PTSD can lead you to make bad decisions, if you are not aware. Triggers can be anywhere, and can pop up unexpectedly. And being triggered can lead you to make a bad decision.

This caused me to make a bad life–changing decision once. I was enrolled in a graduate program in Forestry, and was trying to register when I crossed paths with a very nasty and sadistic University employee who was in charge of registering. I didn't know it then, but this person triggered my PTSD, and I became enraged, walked out, and didn't return. I had also recently lost a part–time lab job there due to cutbacks. I decided these setbacks were "telling me something", and went out and got a job as a Social Worker.

In doing this I walked away from the thing I wanted to do most in life, and later came to regret it. My working life has never been as close to what I am, and all because the PTSD pushed me toward a bad decision. Seeing setbacks as "bad omens" is another result of abuse, as you are always looking for such things (which are not true, but come from your negative perceptions).

Therefore you need to keep in mind that ***PTSD can cause bad decisions***. Always analyze this factor when making important ones, so you can neutralize it. Wait 'till your emotions cool down, and give yourself extra time when this happens. And make sure you *re–focus* on what you *really* want.

Sometimes people with PTSD are happier and do better if they are self-employed. Customers come and go, and if one triggers you, you can turn down the job, or simply wait until it's over.

Why So Much Anxiety?

Sometimes you may have very strong anxiety that doesnt seem to make sense. It seems way out of proportion to what is happening. I get this from some triggers. At the same time, I feel panicky and my head races with any solution that comes to mind. The anxiety worsens, and it feels out of control.

My feeling is that it's a combination of hypervigilance and the emotional component of a trigger. I suspect I'm not the only one who has this problem.

My solution for this so far is to recognize that I'm experiencing PTSD, and that it is not real. Then I do my best to stop focusing on the panic/trigger and engage in a pleasant distraction, whatever seems to work. "What's the worst thing that can happen?" seems to also be a good question to ask yourself, then accept the worst thing happening.

When you have a problem like this, it can be good to consult a website like helpguide.org to get familiar with the latest knowledge about PTSD. This can help you figure out your own solution.

If You Want To Be Kind

And to close this chapter, here are some things to avoid with victims of PTSD:

- Because of our past, we are more sensitive to insults (real or imagined), being made fun of (even as a joke), being laughed at, or a show of disrespect.

- Put–downs and negative criticism can be more hurtful than is usual, and so can aggressive anger.

- We are sensitive to all forms of abuse.

- We have a need to be accepted as we are, and if we are loved, we need it to be the unconditional kind.

- We tend to be more vulnerable to stress than average.

- Some of us are more vulnerable to various forms of addiction (drugs, alcohol, sexual, etc.). That's because we are needy for obvious reasons, whether we let it show or not. Those who have these problems will need help with this too.

- We really appreciate when others are kind, and treat us well.

That said, we can be very good at giving and receiving love, if only because of our need for it, and our awareness of its importance. We can be of strong and good character. And we can be just as good at everything else. We can live good and happy lives once we recover.

Now that we've defined the scope of the problem, we'll talk more about ways of doing something about it in the next section, "Strategies And Tools For Recovery".

Part Four

Now, What To Do?
Strategies And Tools
For Recovery

Here I'll tell you about all the tools and strategies I've picked up over the years. And maybe a few tricks.

These include: Medications, communication skills, standing up to the abuser, and many attitudes, actions and techniques that moved me toward recovery. Every one of them was important for me, and it took many years to learn them all.

Chapter 12

Anti–Depressants And Other Meds

NOTE: Let me stress something here, it's important. I'm not a doctor. Nor am I qualified to prescribe or recommend medication to anyone. So what follows is my own personal experience, and is not medical advice. I share my experience in hopes that it will help you take a careful look at medications, and to help you come up with your own questions for your doctor if and when you use them. I recommend that you always look up whatever medications you are prescribed in the PDR–physician's reference, (usually in your local library) so you know what the medicine is for, how it works, and what the side effects are.

What Is The Science?

So far, to the best of my knowledge as I write, SSRI's

(selective serotonin reuptake inhibitors, which increase the amount of serotonin, a neurotransmitter, in the nerve synapses) are the "standard" treatment for PTSD, specifically Zoloft. Also, propranolol (a beta blocker used for heart problems, tremors and anxiety) has been tried in the past for PTSD in children without clear success. And now there are promising studies on adults taking limited amounts of propranolol for PTSD (note warning ahead).

Medical authorities recognize that there can be some dangers in taking any of these medications for some people, and recommend that they be taken only under medical supervision. I agree.

What Are The Myths?

There are lots of books and celebrities and you–name–its that speak out against taking anti–depressants and, in some cases, any psychoactive medications. These folks give all sorts of reasons, such as:

- They will numb you from pain you *need* to feel

- They will take both pain and joy away and leave you a zombie

- They will interfere with God's natural healing

- They are only for weak people. Strong people can do without them

- They just give you more problems

If you look carefully, you'll find that ***these myths are not put forward by any doctor who is qualified to treat***

PTSD. Unfortunately, these myths *do* play into peoples' fear of the unknown, and may keep many who could benefit away from these medications.

Well, let me be clear: *None of the above myths are true*. SSRI's can and do help many who have PTSD. And propranolol and other meds may turn out to be helpful also.

In fact, I'd say that without some help from an SSRI, I would not have recovered. It put a floor under my PTSD and depression, so that while on the SSRI, my depression was made milder. That, in turn, gave me the energy to do the things I needed to do to recover, instead of fighting every day just to survive.

The thing that really gets me about these myth–weavers is how, without any professional qualifications, they think they know best for everybody else. They usually get around this by saying there is some kind of conspiracy going on, say, between doctors and drug companies. While most doctors don't yet know all they want to know about these problems, they have mostly dedicated their lives trying to help people like us.

We PTSD sufferers are clinging to life, day after day by a fingernail, and these know–it–alls who have no idea what we go through are telling us how precious our pain is, how weak we are, and how God disapproves.

Need I say more?

Fear Of Medication Is Fear Of Having A Problem

As I've said before, it's hard for people to admit they

have something wrong emotionally, so myths like those listed above encourage them to deny the problem. That just prolongs suffering and makes it worse. Sometimes I wonder how many people have died before their time because they were too afraid to admit they had a problem, and so didn't get the help they needed. To me, people who criticize others for getting help they need are as bad as the ones who yell for the suicidal person to jump.

Stigma And Denial

Let's face it. There's a stigma to having a "mental illness", or a "mental disorder". Aside from being "not cool", other people are afraid of it, because people sometimes fear what they don't understand. And we can feel that if we admit we have a "problem", it means we're admitting to being inferior (so it seems to confirm what the abuser said about us). We may be shunned or disrespected by others who know. That's because (lucky for them) they have no understanding of what we go through.

Many people live their whole lives thinking everyone is or should be just like them, and there's nothing you can do about that. And as for the anti–drug folks, I think they are extreme in their beliefs to the point of being irrational. They have no credible science to back them up. You don't have to pay attention to them! Their beliefs reflect their own issues and/or a narrow mind, and have nothing to do with you.

People hurting and disappointing you because that's how some people are, is no excuse for not doing what you need to recover!

The Truth

The truth is that a person who has recovered from a disorder tends to be *more* mature than average, and has their priorities well sorted out. They can actually be more in control of their lives and themselves than most people. They know their strengths, and their limitations, who they are and what they want. And fair–weather friends aren't all that important in a person's life. People's bad reactions can hurt all right, but this is not a good reason to avoid doing what you have to do. And when you are recovered, you can be proud of achieving something very difficult that requires both personal strength and strength of character.

Also, there's an idea out there that anti–depressants like prozac can change you into somebody else, or that they actually do more harm than good. Books have been written saying these things. *Except for very real side effects that everyone should consider (and which require medical supervision); and for some medications, the possibility of dependency or addiction* (not for SSRI's or propranolol)*, these accusations have no scientific basis*.

Any competent doctor will tell you the facts, and will monitor your medication to make sure it is helping you. He will be aware of any dangers, and will change or adjust medication as necessary. I do think it's possible that dosages need to be varied more to fit each patient's biochemistry, which is something the science is beginning to look at.

Finally, you should know that anti–depressants don't work for everyone. I believe the effectiveness is about 75%, which is a rough figure, depending on the report.

What anti-depressants *can* do is let you be yourself —finally! My constant prayer was: "Please, let me have my life back!" Once I was taking my tiny dose of anti-depressant, my wife remarked, "I feel like I have you back again." So did I.

Well, I ask you: Stigma—so what? Isn't it **YOUR** life? Will you let "what people might think" stop you from becoming a recovered, happy person? If you want to heal and recover, you'll have to do everything you can to make that happen. It won't happen by itself. For many people, that will include taking anti–depressant or other medication.

It Changed My Life

When you're in PTSD, you experience intense, powerful, overwhelming negative emotions. Sometimes this can put you right into a depression. And sometimes, the only way to avoid frequent deep depression is to be taking medication.

I'm absolutely sure that without that small amount of anti–depressant, I would not have been able to recover. Before the medication, I was in deep depression, with suicidal urges, a lot of the time. Most of my energy was spent on surviving. It was impossible for me to sustain any long–range goals, or even tackle my problems. Since taking ¼ to ½ the usual dose of an anti-depressant, my life changed dramatically in three ways:

- *First*, my mood has been more level, instead of up and down.

- **Second**, when PTSD strikes, it no longer sends me right into depression every time, and when it does it's milder.

- **Third**, my energy has been freed up so I could both work on my recovery and sustain progress toward my personal goals, as opposed to just trying to survive day to day. It's because of this energy that I've been able to write and publish this book. That's quite a lot of benefit, I think. So if I need medicine, I will use it.

How Antidepressants Work

What do anti–depressants do? They make it so the chemicals in your brain called neurotransmitters are at a high enough level for your brain to function properly. The one I'm familiar with is an SSRI. What that means is it keeps your brain from using up too much of the neurotransmitter serotonin at once, and keeps the level high enough so you don't feel depressed. All it does is make your brain work more efficiently, and avoids a scarcity of an important chemical that protects against depression.

Kind of the way a vitamin supplement works when you have a shortage of that vitamin, only a little more complicated. Nothing very sinister or mysterious or conspiratorial about that, is there? And there is a lot of good science to back this up.

There are also other medications that regulate levels of other neurotransmitters like dopamine, but I'm not familiar with them, and my doctor says they don't help at this time.

There is a medication called trazodone which can sometimes help with sleeping and which may strengthen the effectiveness of SSRI's. I find it only rarely helpful if at all for my own situation.

Who To See About Medication

If you decide to try an anti–depressant, you can see either a *family physician* or a *psychiatrist*. While the psychiatrist is theoretically the most qualified to dispense and monitor the medication, I've had my very worst experiences with psychiatrists, and so have others I know. For some reason, I've had the best luck with family physicians when it comes to medications.

So, what can you do? I would first talk about the problem, with your family physician to see what he/ she recommends. Then I'd ask them if they know of a psychiatrist they feel they can trust. Why? In theory, they should have the most knowledge to give you a correct diagnosis, and correct, up to date treatment, including medication.

But **be warned**. I know personally of someone who was taken off a medication known to cause severe with-drawal, and also given a mixture of new ones known to have severe side affects. It could have killed him. And this by a Psychiatrist!

So be careful about going on or off medications. I think common sense says you shouldn't add more than one medication at a time. If someone recommends you do, ask questions, and check with your family physician!

Just don't put it off! You may want to keep in mind that sometimes, doses as low as ¼ of normal are considered a "minimum effective dose" (this information is available in medical journals, and can be referenced by any doctor).

Many of these medications can have strong and discomforting side effects. We are all different in the way medication affects us, so you need a doctor who will inform you about any dangers, and who will monitor your progress.

If you try anti–depressants, have patience. It takes at least 10 days to two weeks or more for some medications to work. It may take some trial and error for your doctor to find one that works for you, and to adjust the dose so it's effective with a minimum of side effects. But it can be worth the trouble. Freedom from depression and energy to spare are worth a little effort, aren't they?

Do What's Best For You!

I'm sure I couldn't have recovered without the help of medication. That makes me think that for many, it may be required for recovery. So be smart, and do what you have to do—and be careful about it.

Anxiety Medications

The following are my own experience and should not affect your personal choices, made with your doctor:

Tranquilizers

For me, at least, taking a tranquilizer (such as Valium) never did me any good. They seemed to help at first, then I had to keep increasing the dose. Then, when I had to stop, there was a really bad withdrawal.

Xanax

I found this to be a helpful, *very occasional* medication for anxiety, but not the best. I felt drugged when I took it, which I found unpleasant.

Klonopin

This is a very powerful medication that I never took. Someone in my family did, and they have had withdrawal problems (with panic disorder). They haven't been able to stop taking it. But it does help them, and it is still recomended by their doctor.

Propranolol—It Works For Me

There is recent research that suggests that this drug can have dramatic good effects on some kinds of PTSD. Learning this, I tried it, and found it *(for me)* to be the best anti-anxiety drug.

VERY IMPORTANT: Some people cannot safely take this drug, and you may have to have an electrocardiogram and possibly other tests by

a doctor to be cleared to take it. If your doctor prescribes it, ask him if he's sure it's safe.

What the drug does is to slow or stop the production of adrenaline, which is a factor in anxiety. It's hard to be anxious with no adrenaline. I use this drug when needed and it works really well for me.

Explore It With Your Doctor!

So that's *my own personal experience (not medical advice)*.

I don't know if my personal experience (which is not science) will help you very much, but *I offer it to show you that we each need to find what, if any, meds will help us personally*. You can only find that with the help of a good, sensible and knowledgeable doctor.

I guess my best *personal* advice would be to find a family doctor who is good at medications, double check what they are doing by researching the PDR and asking a pharmacist, and be careful about every step. Then judge for yourself if they are helping you. If not, try another re-comended doctor, or medication, until you find one that can help you. Be especially careful about major medication or dosage changes!

Now we'll talk about another important tool for recovery, and one that will improve and enhance all your relationships with others: The art of being a good communicator.

Chapter Thirteen

How To Be A Good Communicator

If you ask the average person what "good communication" is, they'd probably say "when I get my point across", or "when I get someone to listen to what I'm saying". And that would be absolutely wrong!

Here's the big secret: ***Communication is about listening***. It's about two people listening to each other, ***and hearing*** what each other is saying. It's a two–way thing. And it's not as easy as you might think, because it can defy your personal logic. You have to learn how to do this.

Others Don't Think Exactly Like Us

Why do we need to learn how to do this? Why isn't it natural? Because we all see and feel about things differently, and we don't realize it. Why? For one thing, we're all born with, and learn to have, different personality traits. And for another, we all have different life experiences.

It can be hard to understand the thoughts and feelings of someone with different traits and experiences (which can be anybody, including your spouse or child).

Truth is, *most of us believe everybody thinks like we do*, so we tend to project our own thoughts and feelings onto others. And we may refuse to believe we're wrong.

This was driven home to me when I practiced family therapy in child welfare. My biggest job was to say, "did you hear what your (husband, wife, child, parent) just said?" So many times they did not hear! My next job was to help the person speaking convince the other person that yes, they really did feel or think what they had just said.

Then the listener would often say, "No, you don't feel/think that". Or they would say, "You mean you feel/think *that*? I don't believe you". Why did this happen? Because the listener didn't feel/think that way, so they couldn't imagine that anyone else could.

One of the great myths of marriage and parenthood is that the other person knows exactly what you think and feel, and understands you completely. This is absolutely not true, and it's the reason we all need to learn effective communication. Many of our relationship problems come from bad communication. We may be the same as others in some ways, but we are all different in *many* ways.

For people with PTSD, good communication is *vital* to recovery and your important relationships.

How To Learn To Communicate

The standard communication exercise used in family

or marital therapy goes like this: The participants each take a turn at saying what they feel/think about a problem they are having.

First, one person speaks, while the other listens. Then the other repeats what the speaker said like this: "Are you saying ......?" Then the speaker either says yes or no, and if no, they repeat what they said in a slightly different way. Then the listener again asks, "are you saying..?" until it's clear that the listener has heard it all correctly. The listener is encouraged to accept what the speaker says as true, even though what is said may be outside their experience and understanding. Then the positions are reversed, and the listener is now the speaker, etc.

In this way, you listen to each other, and most people are surprised at some of the things that come out in the open, where they can now be dealt with. This leads to greater intimacy and understanding in a family, and tends to bring everyone closer together. It helps the family solve their problems in a realistic way that works for all.

There are a few rules. No attacking, no shouting, no cursing, no arguing, etc. And you must listen when it is your turn to do so, and try to accept what the other person is telling you, once you can hear it.

An Example

Here's a little example of how this can work:

Person # 1: When you make jokes about my appearance it hurts me.

Person # 2: Are you saying that when I make a joke you are too sensitive, and it makes you feel bad?

Person # 1: What I'm saying is that when you joke about my appearance, it makes me feel that you don't love me anymore.

Person # 2: Are you saying that when I joke like that you feel I don't love you?

Person # 1: Yes, when you joke like that I feel you don't love me.

Person # 2: I'm sorry, I didn't know it made you feel that way. I will try not to joke about that from now on. I do love you, and didn't realize how it made you feel. I would never intentionally hurt you.

Note in this example that the listener first puts an incorrect spin on the teller's statement, and subtly accuses the teller of being "too sensitive", probably because such jokes do not bother the listener. But when the listener understands the fear underlying the teller's feeling, they can realize why the teller was hurt, and that they didn't mean to cause that feeling. They can then reassure the teller by speaking to their fear, and by promising to try to avoid repeating the mistake.

Problem solved, and everyone walks away feeling better, and closer to each other. Notice that ***without verification, there is no communication***. The "Are you saying" part is the key.

As you may see by now, real communication requires that both people learn to *listen to each other*. This can be hard to do by yourselves, if you haven't been getting along well. It will be too tempting to shut the other one out, or to go on the attack. It will probably help to do this with a professional at first, to get the feel of it and to learn how to avoid falling into the old ruts.

While it may be hard to learn at first, it will become much easier later. And once you learn how you never forget. The best ones to help you learn this are those who specialize in *family therapy*, and some MSW social workers are very good at this.

Communication skills are very important when there is PTSD present, because a person in PTSD is not in the reality of the present moment. Letting them say their feelings will make both people more aware of the sufferer's reality when they are in PTSD. And it can highlight for both people the two different realities (real vs. "PTSD real"). This can shine a light on what the problems are, and point toward solutions. It can take a lot of stress out of all family relationships, and it fosters healing and recovery. It's a tool you don't want to do without.

Now let's talk about another very powerful tool for healing. We'll discuss how and when to Stand Up to your abusing parent(s).

Chapter Fourteen

Standing Up To The Abuser

In this chapter, I'll tell you how I "Stood Up" to my abuser(s). I got some of the ideas for doing this from a few books: 1)"Toxic Parents–Overcoming Their Hurtful Legacy And Reclaiming Your Life", by Dr. Susan Forward, Bantam Books, 1989. 2) "Games People Play", by Eric Berne, Random House, 1964. 3) "I'm O.K., You're O.K.", by Thomas Harris, M.D., Harper Collins, 1967.

As mentioned before, I used some of the ideas from these books and from other places, and from my training and experience, to help form my own unique methods for my recovery. I rejected what didn't fit me. And I recommend you do the same, including with this book! One size does not fit all, and we each have to find our own way.

Read and study the above books, and anything you can find that may help! I'll mention where I agree or disagree with the above sources to show you what I mean by finding your own way.

What follows here is strictly about my own personal experience with "standing up". I share it, as with all else in this book, in case it can be some help to you. *I had to handle my buried anger before I could do it.* Also, *I had to remember the major incidents of my abuse.* And you must take responsibility, with help from your good therapist, as to how or whether any of my experiences apply to you.

What I like to call "*standing up to your abuser*" is how I put an end to the abusive relationship for good, felt better about myself, gained self respect, and began a new and healthier relationship with my abuser(s) (at first I didn't know if there would be a relationship). Dr. Forward calls this "Confrontation", but that doesn't describe what I did. The primary dictionary definitions of that word involve anger, hostility, fighting and arguing. And in my opinion, that is absolutely not how this process works, and is not the frame of mind I was in.

I did it strictly in an adult way. I told my abuser(s) how I recalled they hurt me, what I remembered feeling when it happened, and the impact it seemed to have on my life (these are similar to Dr. Forward"s first three of the four steps she recommends for "Confrontation". I didn't think it was right for me to use her fourth step, telling the abuser what you want them to do about it).

I did this for each major incident of abuse that I remembered.

I would think anyone who decided to try their own version of this would want *help from a therapist* to help handle the emotions it can bring out, and so they could remain in "adult mode" (I'll explain soon).

It was a surprise to the abuser, and they reacted with strong emotion and defensiveness. That was O.K., because this exercise was meant to free me from ***my*** part of the abusive relationship. It also gave my abuser a chance to change their way of relating to me. But it was mainly to help me recover.

Here are examples of standing up the wrong way and the right way:

- *Standing Up the wrong way: "You *@#&!! You ruined my life! I hate you!"*

- *Standing Up the right way: "When I was 10 yrs. old, you accused me of stealing your money. You yelled, hit me, and called me bad names for hours, and almost had me believing I had done it. Then my sister confessed, and you comforted her, leaving me all torn apart, with you still acting as though it had been me.*

- *This made me feel you didn't care about me at all, and you didn't even apologize. It made me feel that I was nothing, and that no one loved me. I still feel these things to this day, and this and other incidents like it contributed to my illness/unhappiness."*

It's Done In An Adult Way

Can you see the difference? One is purely emotional, like a child would say it, and the other is adult and rational. This true incident was part of my own standing up to my parents. In this chapter, I'll tell you how I believe I did it the right way, in case you decide *with your therapist* to do your own version.

I Had To Prepare

Standing Up is not as simple as it sounds. It was not about complaining, or about reading someone the riot act. And it was not about giving back what I got. I had to be well prepared, both emotionally and with the things I had to say. And I had to know the right way to say them. Standing up is a well planned exercise that if done right, can lead to healing and recovery. It may even help the abusing parent to move in a more positive direction (which was their choice, not mine). If I couldn't have "stayed in my adult" (see below), it will probably not have helped. I had to be prepared for what was likely to happen, and be enough in control of my emotions that I could *behave as an adult*, if it was to work well or accomplish anything.

Since my abuser was not expecting this, they were naturally very defensive. That would probably happen in most cases, and it took time for me to know the final outcome.

How It Worked

Before we get into the mechanics of Standing Up, I'd like to tell you how it helped, and what it did for me.

The biggest thing I did was to **Stand Up For Myself** with my abusing parent(s). I did this *not just as an adult, but in an adult way*. This is something I could never do as an abused child, and that made it very powerful. No matter what my parent said or did, standing up this way released me from the past, and gave me more power as an adult.

In facing them I stated in no uncertain terms how I recalled they hurt me, what I remembered feeling when it happened, and the impact it seemed to have on me.

In an adult way, I put all those fears and all the anger out on the table, in the open. There was nothing to hide or hide from any more. It was my own declaration of independence. From that point on, we would never go back to the way it was, and we were all free to move forward into healing, happiness and fulfillment, if we chose to.

Thus healing took place regardless of what my parents said, or how they reacted.

What It Did For Me

In my case, Standing Up not only changed the way I felt about myself and my parents, but it eventually also changed the way my parents felt, and how they related to me. My mom had already apologized for what she had done, and was at first puzzled by my need for this. Later she said she understood I had to do it for myself.

Standing up to them, I was finally released from some of the anger and fears of childhood (which I had always felt around them), and could leave them behind. That made it so I could later relate to my parents in a loving, adult way. It was the hammer that shattered many barriers from the past. It also enabled my parents to face the fact that they had harmed me, and move on to a more loving relationship as well.

I Was Lucky

I think I am fortunate it turned out that way, and for this to happen, it required all of us to try hard. ***This will not happen for everyone***, as some parents will not be capable of facing what they did. But even if the best doesn't happen, one can still be freed from the past, and can move on to a much better life.

How I Did It

Now let's talk about how I Stood Up.

First, I Got Ready

First, the preparation. To be successful and have a positive result, I had to learn and practice how to "*be in my adult*". Most people will need the help of a therapist.

Here's where the books by Eric Berne and Thomas Harris, M.D., which I'd read many years before, helped me. I still remembered the lessons in these books.

In "*Games People Play*", Berne, a founder of Transactional Analysis explains the human personality in terms of 1) the parent part, which is an emotional part that acts like a judgmental or nurturing parent, 2) the child part, which is also emotional and contains your childhood fears and other feelings, and 3) the adult part, which uses the cognitive, thinking part of the brain to make objective, unemotional choices and decisions. The book also shows the many ways people interact based on this theory.

The second book further clarifies and explains about parent, adult and child.

These books have good examples of what the parent, child and adult in your head sound like. Here is my own example of each that helped me understand this:

- *(Harsh) Parent* – *"You never do anything right! You're such an idiot!"*

- *(Needy) Child* – *"Oh, I feel so alone! I need someone to take care of me!"*

- *(Objective) Adult* – *"I notice I'm feeling anxious. Maybe I should try going for a walk".*

I've noticed we say things like that to ourselves, and sometimes to others. Notice that the "adult" is objective and unemotional. The "parent" can also say soothing things, but it usually is harsh to abuse victims.

So for me, *"staying in my adult"* meant remaining objective, level–headed, and as unemotional and calm as possible. I spoke reason, not emotion. Ironic, isn't it? ***In order to free my emotions, I had to perform an exercise of reason and restraint.***

I think that many would need the support of a good therapist to do this right. The emotions I felt toward my abuser were raw and very strong. And before I could do this, I **absolutely** had to resolve my hidden anger first.

So I knew I'd have to resolve my hidden anger and be confident I could stay in my adult, no matter what the abuser(s) might throw at me (and there *were* a lot of negatives thrown). When I was prepared for all that, I was ready to leave the past behind, and to change how I felt about and related to my abuser(s).

Kindness

One thing I tried to include in standing up was an attitude of kindness. Kindness is not giving in, or weakness, or even forgiveness. In fact, it was hard at times to be kind to people who had hurt me in so many ways. Some people reading this may feel it's outrageous to show any mercy to the abuser.

But this was not done to hurt my parents or get even. If this had been my goal, my standing up would have failed. It was done to free myself from the past, so I could move on to better things. Somehow I knew that real happiness includes an attitude of kindness.

Soon we'll talk about *mindfuness*, which I've found to be an important way of keeping free from the past. And kindness to yourself and others is a part of that way of living. I was convinced that the more I could be kind while standing up, the more chance there was for a better future relationship with the abusers, if that was possible.

The best I could do was to not shout or get angry. I just stood there and let my parents' hostility run off me like water off a duck's back. Doing the best I could with this was enough (as it usually is with anything).

Things I Kept In Mind

I had to be ready to respond to whatever my parent said or did in an objective and adult way. In other words, no matter what bait they dangled in front of me, I didn't take it, but remained calm, objective, and "on message". When I couldn't stay in my adult, I said nothing.

To do this I had to be prepared for all the **negatives** the abuser(s) were likely to throw at me, and for the possibility that standing up might end our relationship. And I had to remember that I didn't deserve the abuse (I'd already learned that lesson from a good therapist). I think that while I may still have had some "child type" feelings of responsibility, I was clear in my "reasoning" mind that I was not at fault, and I was stubborn about that.

Most important was practice, practice, practice.

My Standing Up

So I practiced, was ready, and got what support I could. I went to my parents' house and said: "There's something I have to talk to you about". Then I went through a handful of incidents that had affected me the most. For each incident I said: X is the act that hurt me. Y is how I remember feeling when you did it. Z is how it has seemed to impact me and my life.

I did this in a calm, adult manner. So, for example, as I told my mother: *"You called me into the kitchen, saying "I want to talk to you". I thought it would be something nice. Then you said, "We have decided to send you away".*

This hurt me more than anything else you ever did. I felt that you were abandoning me, and I was only eight or nine years old. I felt that I no longer had a home. This crushed my spirit, and contributed to my being mentally ill from then on. It hurt me deeply".

Then, I continued, going through each major incident of abuse.

What The Abusers Did

One thing first. It has occurred to me that during my standing up, I never felt I was in physical danger. If it had become dangerous, I would have followed a motto at an old social work employer: "When in doubt, get the hell out"! If a face–to–face had not worked out, I would have done "two chair" therapy (see below) .

My parents reacted defensively. They told me why it was right to do these things, and tried to turn it back on me. I expected it. Think about it: This was a surprise to them. They were not prepared, like I was. So of course, they reverted to what worked on me in the past. They tried to intimidate me. They "explained" why they had to "discipline" me, and why I "deserved it" (I did not). When these things happened, I remained in adult mode. *I did not rise to the bait*, nor was I fazed by any of it. My parents insisted that I needed "discipline", and that I was an "obnoxious kid", and deserved it all. I just calmly continued on.

My mother, who had apologized a few years earlier, asked "When will this be over?" I replied that I didn't know, and had the thought: "It will be over when it's over for me". She also asked: "Was it all bad? Wasn't there anything good?" To which I replied: "Yes, there was a lot of good, but that's not what I need to talk about today".

When I was finished, the air was so thick you could have cut it with a knife. My dad was yelling, "Parent abuse, parent abuse!" I then turned and quietly left. I remember feeling many things: Emotional exhaustion, sadness, and a feeling that, *whatever happened now, the past was over, and it was time for a new beginning.* I felt that my relationship with my parents might be over for good, but what really mattered was that I had finally stood up for myself. I felt released, free. And sad, because I knew I might never see them again. Something had died, and I later realized it was the old abusive relationship. That was a good thing.

What Happened After

Well, my parents surprised me. After a period of time for all of us to absorb the lessons of Standing Up, my parents reached out to me, and without re–hashing or further apologizing, we embarked on a new and truly loving relationship, which lasted throughout both their lives. My mother reverted back to her old behavior just once after that, and when she did I stopped her and said *"You can never speak to me like that again"*, and walked out. We were back together soon after, and it never happened again.

I think that Standing Up made this possible, and I knew that whatever my parents might do, I must never again allow myself to take the blame for what they did, or minimize it. To recover, I had to first focus on the bad things they did, *until I stood up for myself.* Only after that was it O.K. to open my heart to them.

It was very important not to *prematurely* forgive them until I was **sure** it was right, and **never** just because I want them to love me. It took time to know how it would go, but I could **never go back on my declaration of independence** in order to gain their approval! Doing so would have aborted my recovery, as I see it. I'll go into more detail about forgiving in a later chapter.

I also knew that whatever my parents decided, I would move on to a better life, with or without them. I could not control what they would do, and I had to take full responsibility for my life going forward.

What If I Couldn't Meet With The Abuser?

If my abusers had died, or were too sick to go through something like this; if they had refused to see me; or if for some reason, I couldn't see them, there was something else I could have done.

I could have done an "empty chair", or "gestalt" therapy. With your therapist there, you speak to an empty chair, as though the abuser were sitting there. You may be very surprised to know that this can be as effective as though the person was actually there! I know this, because it was used for me to deal with my suicidal urges many years ago.

Conclusions

Here are some of my conclusions about Standing Up done right:

- *The power and healing came from standing up for myself in a way I never could as a child*

- *It was a way to resolve many of my resultant feelings from abuse*

- *It helped end the hidden (past) anger I felt toward my parent(s)*

- *It freed me to move on to a better life, and leave the past behind*

- *It changed my relationship with my parents, which in my case became better (that depended on our mutual choices)*

- *I had to see my parent(s) as responsible for the abuse (at least in the "adult" part of my mind) in order for this to work.*

I Never Went Back To The Old Ways

Later, we will discuss things like: To forgive or not, to reconcile or not.

I just know that *there must not be a bribe, or a price* for doing these things. Once I stood up for myself and declared my independence, I could never go back to old ways. I stood firm on this, good things happened, and I moved on to a better life.

I remember an intense period of sadness and grieving after standing up to them, as though somebody had died. What I learned later was that what had died, *needed* to die—the old abuser–victim relationship. Only then was I in any way capable of a real and loving relationship with my parents.

As we continue, we'll talk about some solid, effective ways to make life better and to help with depression and PTSD that I've learned over the years. Each of the things I'll tell you about is a major tool in my happiness toolbox.

Chapter 15

The Bad Parent In Your Head

If you've had an abusive childhood, there will be things you say to yourself all the time that keep you down, in pain, and away from recovery. This is not a maybe, it's guaranteed! We've talked before about how young children who are abused absolutely believe the bad things their parents say about them.

The really sad thing is that they wind up saying those same things to themselves. That's a real nightmare for the adult child of abusive parents. In a sense, your parent sits in your head and keeps abusing you when they're no longer there. ***You've been trained to go on abusing yourself***, and will continue this until you recognize it and learn how to stop it.

Clearly, this leads to "locking in" a bad self–image. To make matters worse, the *negative thinking actually makes more bad things happen*. You can become a self–abusing unhappiness machine. Somehow you need to get from this bad place to knowing and believing in your unconditional worth, and being able to unconditionally love yourself.

How To Stop Abusing Yourself

For me, the way out of this kind of thinking requires three things:

- Recognizing and knowing when you are saying bad things to yourself.
- Countering this each time with the truth.
- Replacing the negative thing you're saying/thinking with a positive thing that is undeniably true.

When you recognize your thinking, you become more aware of its effects. When you replace a negative thought with a true positive thought, you are learning to feel better about yourself, and to get negative thinking under control.

Some Things We Say

Let's go through some of the more common examples of things abuse survivors say to themselves, and see how to handle them. Refer back to chapter 6, "What Abuse Makes You Feel About Yourself", if you need to refresh on how you learned to think this way.

"I'm Bad/No Good"

It's likely you were told this many times, in many ways. And you came to believe it, because the parent–gods knew all (or so we all believe when we're very young). But was it really true? If you look back, you will probably remember either trying very hard to please your parents, or giving up at some point, feeling hopeless. Do you remember your love and joy being returned with pain and punishment? Do you remember feeling shocked, surprised, hurt by the way you were treated?

We Need Unconditional Love

One of the biggest jobs a parent has is to create an atmosphere of trust and unconditional love. Did your parents do that for you? Did they tell you they loved you, how wonderful you were, how good you were? That's what healthy, loving parents do. Or did they tell you things that were very different?

How many truly bad people are there? Not many. Usually they had no love in their life, came not to care about others at all, and as a result, made bad choices they thought made sense. Or they are sociopaths or psychopaths. These types are usually missing a piece of their humanity, and are a small minority. If you care about others, you are not one of them. To get a perspective on this, go to a busy hospital nursery, and see if you can pick out the bad babies. We're mostly all pretty wonderful when we start out. And that never really changes.

If you look carefully, you'll find plenty of evidence that you are not "bad". One result of abuse can be *perfectionism*. If only you could be perfect, then you'd be "good enough", and loved. Of course, perfection is not possible, but trying to be perfect can lead to lots of pain and frustration.

Why You Feel You're Bad

So why do you sometimes feel that you are bad? As a small child, when parents say and treat you like you're bad, you tend to think *"My parents don't love me, so I must be bad. It's my fault that they don't love me. I'm no good."* You've then internalized badness. So now when something goes wrong, you blame yourself. You even blame yourself for the abuse! While you may fight and feel wronged, you also come to believe you deserve it. You may then come to fear your "badness", and try to hide it. You are afraid it will get out, people will know. That's how it was for me.

You may even succeed at hiding this from yourself, but you can't hide the fear, which will be background music in your feelings. Abuse–caused lack of self esteem is really a nasty web that's woven around and through you.

You Can Change It

Once you become aware you are seeing things this way, you can begin to change it, as I did.

Each time you say "I'm bad", think, is that really true? Are you kind, generous, caring? What are some of the good things about you? Make a list! You'll find you're pretty decent if you look closely. Find the evidence that you're not bad, then replace the "I'm bad" with "I'm a good person, because....". When you truly grasp what your parents have done to you with this, you will be outraged and angry (anger was dangerous in early childhood). That's good, because as I've said before, you need to recognize this anger, bring it into consciousness (with help), and heal it.

Another belief you can pick up from abuse is, *"No matter how hard I try, it's never good enough"*.

You Could Never Please Them

I remember proudly bringing home a report card with all A's except for a B in phys. ed. When I showed it to my father, he said: "Why did you get a B?" Boy, did that feel bad.

It was probably true that you couldn't please your abusing parent(s) in childhood, but the *belief* that no matter what you do, it's never good enough makes an *adult* tend to give up before they try very hard. The adult child of abuse will take the first sign of difficulty or discouragement as proof that the thing is hopeless, and will give up prematurely. He will also fear failure as proof of his being no good. This does not lead to a lot of achievement in life.

It's natural that you'd feel this way if no matter what you did, you could never please your parent(s). As with all the other mental remnants from abuse, ***it's not your fault you feel these things***. Anybody would. Your job is to get some of this stuff out of your head and replace it with good things, so you can go on and have a good life

What You Can Do

Again, the way out of this is to first *recognize* you believe that no matter how hard you try, it won't be good enough. *Learn to see it while it's happening*. Then realize that your best *is* always good enough. It has to be, because we can't do better than our best. We'll make mistakes, and screw things up sometimes, but if we keep trying and learning, we will eventually succeed at what we're trying to do, most of the time.

One thing I say to myself a lot: *"Your best is good enough"*. Also: *"The road to success is paved with mistakes and failures"*. These things are true in real adult life. You get places by having goals, and persisting until you achieve a good part of them. And you must take risks and make mistakes to achieve anything of value! ***Making mistakes is O.K., even necessary!*** Persistence and hard, steady thoughtful work will beat unrefined superior talent every time. There are success mechanisms in our minds that we can learn to tap into, and I'll talk more about them later.

What You Can Do Next

Once you've recognized your "not good enough" belief, and realized where it came from, and that it's not true for you as an adult, you can start reaching for your dreams. First, you dream. Then you see yourself achieving your dreams. Then you set goals, and attack them with relish, one by one. You then keep going, possibly adjusting, but not giving up your dreams, until they are yours. In this way, adult children of abuse can learn to switch from "never be good enough" to "I can achieve much of what I dream and work for, if I don't give up". We'll talk more about setting goals, and achievement for self, later.

Another thing the abused believe: *"People don't like me/pick on me/abandon me"*.

It Wasn't Exactly Paranoia, But It's Over

If people are really after you, it's not paranoia. And as an abused child, someone *was* after you—the abuser. And the one after you was supposed to love, protect and nurture you. That's a pretty major betrayal, isn't it? Is it surprising that after going through that, you would tend to see malice in other people, and have difficulty trusting them and feeling comfortable with them (especially new people)?

We tend to see the present through the lens of our past experience. It will help in your relationships with others when you are able to see with complete clarity that what your abuser did to you was **wrong, and not your fault**. Then it will be a little easier for others to earn your trust (but don't be surprised if trust is a problem for you). The truth is, the past is over. Now you have to learn, as much as you can, to stop carrying it around inside you.

How I Got Free

Getting out of dysfunctional beliefs requires seeing clearly what really happened, what that did to you, and that you were not responsible for it happening. Remembering truthfully what happened, and tying that to how these things affected you is like putting pieces of a puzzle together. Each piece means little by itself, but the picture becomes clear when the pieces are all in place.

If you have trouble perceiving present reality because of past bad experience, it helps to have a good therapist guiding you towards adult reality. They can help you keep focused and can suggest alternate behaviors for specific problems.

Other People Aren't That Into Us

And what is the truth about most other people? First, *they barely notice you, because they're concerned with their own problems!* Most of them are pretty nice. And everyone makes mistakes, says things wrong, and has bad days, which usually means nothing. It helps to cut yourself and everyone else plenty of slack. Usually, the innocent motive is the correct one. And if someone behaves in a nasty way, it means *they* have a problem that has nothing to do with you.

There are a few sadistic folks out there (with bad problems of their own), who may catch the vibes of your fears, and attempt to engage you in their own pathology. You can learn to ignore these few people, and avoid them if you choose.

Another belief: *"I must please others in order to be loved"*.

Trying To Be Someone Else

Trying to be someone else was something I had to do to survive in childhood, and a big problem in adulthood. *But I could't do it. I could only be myself.*

Some results of this attitude can be following the wrong career; putting yourself last, or not at all; doing things you can't stand all the time; feeling a need to rescue others and to sacrifice yourself.

This is due to a mixture of things: One is the *belief in your own worthlessness*. Another is *fear of being abandoned*, fear of losing someone you care about. You have no trouble convincing yourself that what you really want is foolish, impractical, or not worth the effort. And you are afraid to assert yourself, fearing abandonment. Thus you are defeated from the start.

Here's some news: **We all have a right to live our own life!** People who give and love the best, also love and give to themselves. You can't give much from an empty tank. The truth is, you love and are loved best only after you've learned to live your own life and please yourself. It's who you are. And it makes you nicer and more fun to be around. Jesus said: *"Love your neighbor as yourself"*, which I think is very true. To me it means you have to love yourself first before you can love your neighbor.

Stop The Bad Words

There are other bad things we say to ourselves, which are usually echoes of what the abusive parent said. And if you don't learn to stop thinking these things, you may find yourself saying them to your children. They are false labels that are hard to remove, but must be put to rest. Words like *"lazy"*, or *"bum"*, or *"slut"*, or *"rotten"*. Or worse ones, with four letters. You heard them enough times, and you believe them. They have become part of how you see yourself, and they are wrong!

As before, you must first notice you are doing this. Then ask, what is the truth? Then you substitute a positive, friendly word for the bad one. With practice, you can learn to change this way of thinking. You don't deserve the bad words, you deserve the good ones!

Cognitive Behavioral Therapy

Everything in this chapter describes what I went through and how I learned to quiet the bad parent in my head.

Some of the methods I've just described are part of Cognitive Behavioral Therapy, which we've discussed. This therapy is recognized by science as the most effective one for problems such as PTSD and depression. In general, it focuses on your beliefs and attitudes that cause you to have more negative thoughts, more anxiety, etc. Then it teaches you ways of changing those beliefs and attitudes, so you can lessen your suffering.

In the next chapter, I'll tell you more about how I changed a bad self–image.

Chapter Sixteen

Changing A Bad Self Image

A big part of my problem was how I saw myself, and felt about myself. When the most important people in your early life tell you you're worthless garbage, and you believe it, *this becomes how you see and feel about yourself.* And you believe it because it's your own parent saying so.

You've been convinced that you're one step below a worm. You're likely to deny it, but deep down, you feel it. Consciously or unconsciously, you're afraid of the next bit of proof that seems to show it's true. And you're always seeing that proof, even making it happen (the power of negativity).

It helped when I could understand that I felt this way because of what had been done to me, and not because it was true. It also helped when I learned that attitudes make more of the same, both good and bad, and that we all have the power to change these attitudes if we want to.

Ways To Change Those Bad Feelings

So if someone else had planted bad attitudes in my mind and psyche, I could replace them with ones that would support happiness and growth. This is the opposite of a victim mentality. It means you can have more control over your life if you choose to. And you can change it, though not easily. What follows now are some ways of thinking and behaving that helped me make that change.

Try To Do The Right Thing—Always

Always try to do the right thing, and the thing that is good for you. Try not to do the wrong thing, and the thing that is bad for you. Sounds too simple, but it's not simple when your fears, anger or PTSD are raging. Do the right thing even if it is very hard, even when you don't want to do it. If we think about it, we all usually know what the right thing is, and when we're not sure, we have a good idea what to try. And if you make a mistake, you can learn from it, and try to do better.

When you do the right thing, you can feel good about yourself for having the strength and good sense to do it. And if you do this day after day, it helps you to see yourself as good, and feel some self-worth. And one good thing leads to another.

We're talking about everyday choices: *Get help, or not. Drink too much, or not. Ask that nice person for a date, or not. Push yourself to get moving and do something fun with your child, or stay lost in a fog of self-absorption. Try medications that may help, or not. Hit someone, or not.*

Lose your temper, or go for a long walk to cool down. Hurt someone you love, or not.

Your feelings may be pushing you toward doing something bad, or not doing something good. Many times you can be strong, and do the right thing. You may not feel like dragging yourself out of bed, but you can choose to get up and go to work anyway. You may be feeling afraid of talking to that nice person you're attracted to, but you can choose to go ahead anyway. You may be very angry and about to say terrible things to someone, but you can choose to go out for a walk instead.

Every time you do something like this, you can be proud of your strength and good judgment, and you're building a better self–image. Eventually, you can no longer deny that you're really a pretty good person, of good, strong character. You can actually *earn* a better self–image by just taking care of yourself, and those you love. It's O.K. if you can't do it sometimes. What matters is what happens most of the time, and that you don't stop trying.

Notice Your Good Points

When you're feeling down on yourself, ask, "What is good about me?" What have I done I can be proud of? Have I been kind to others? Do I do good work? What are some of my good qualities? Compassion? Sensitivity? Generosity? Other qualities? Do you have a special talent? Does someone love you? If so, why? Trust me, there are reasons. Are you smart? Friendly? Fun (when not depressed)? Do you have a sense of humor? Have you borne your pain with dignity and courage? Do you have love in your heart?

If you were abused, you will have bad feelings about yourself because of the abuse. So you have to counter that, and a good way is to take honest stock of your goodness on a regular basis. In other words, to remind yourself what you really are, and that you are not what they said you were. The feelings that result from abuse run very deep, and you may always feel them to some extent. But the more you "re–train" yourself to feel good things, the more you'll get into the habit of feeling good.

We All Started Out Wonderful—And We Still Are!

All children are born as wonderful people, and it's a parent's job to tell them so. If that didn't happen for you, then *somebody wasn't doing their job*! So it becomes *your* job to find the wonderful in yourself, and keep telling yourself about it. When you find the wonderful in yourself, you'll be able to see the wonderful in other people.

You're still here, so you've survived so far, and you can be proud of that. All you accomplish toward your recovery, you can be proud of. And you can be proud if you make the *choice* to survive and recover, and *act* on it. It isn't easy to have this elephant on your back and keep on walking. Survivors are heroes for all of us, because they face up to the really hard stuff. Then we look at them and say: "**If they can do it, I can too!** " So you may even be or become a hero to someone.

Turn Negative Into Positive

I turned some of the worst things my parent(s) said

into positive mantras or phrases I repeated that helped me feel better. For example:

"My best is always good enough!" Most regular people know this. How can you do better than your best? Your "best" will vary in different situations, because you're human. The important question is: Have I pleased myself with my effort? Is it good enough for me, today? A related one would be:

"Perfection is not human! My best is just fine." Perfectionism comes from trying to please the abusing parent, which was (and is) impossible. When you try to be perfect, you are still trying to please that parent. They certainly *should* have been pleased. Heck, you probably deserved an award!

"If we don't make mistakes, we'll never learn anything or get anywhere." Also: "The road to success is paved with failures and mistakes." Abuse victims are afraid of making mistakes or failing, because mistakes had terrible consequences. This can kill your initiative and ambition. In the real world, mistakes and failures are expected. What counts is whether or not you learn from them. Then you can step up to the plate and take another swing.

"Actually I'm good at _____; I'm a good person when it comes to _____." Stop accepting the belief that you're no good! Challenge it every chance you get! When you catch yourself thinking, "I'm a (bad thing)", counter it with a good thing you know you are. Don't allow the abuser in your mind to keep belittling you any more.

The Fight Inside Your Head

Do you get the idea? You have to stand up and *fight* for yourself inside your own head. I learned how to root out the negative attitudes I was given, and how to replace them with good attitudes that support my happiness. You do this by *fighting back* in this way, over and over. Is it easy? Not really. But it works, and keeps improving things the more you do it. And repeated thoughts tend to become automatic after a while.

If you want to recover and heal, you'll have to fight for it! Sometimes you'll feel that you can't go on. *So you go on anyway*! If my recovery proves anything, it's that if you keep trying and don't give up, you can make it. Expect some really rough and painful days. And some really good days.

All I can tell you is, it's worth it! To finally find joy in living is worth what it takes to get there. *What else do you have to do that's more important?* Yes, it's unfair that this gets dumped on us, and we have to fix it. But that's the way it is. With hard work, help and a little luck, you may come to agree with something I think often: Be grateful for and enjoy fully every good thing in your life!

Now I want to talk about one of the most powerful tools of all. One that I think saved my life. And that is, how our minds process positive and negative thoughts and attitudes.

Chapter Seventeen

Positive And Negative

This May Have Saved My Life!

In 1980, life for me had become about as bad as it could get. My depression was severe and out of control. It was deeper and longer–lasting than it had ever been, going on for weeks at a time. I was becoming more and more suicidal, and it seemed I wouldn't be able to go on much longer. It was hard to work, and hard to live. One day I was browsing in a bookstore, and a title jumped out at me: "Grow Rich With Peace Of Mind", by Napoleon Hill. I guess it was the "peace of mind" part that pulled at me, because I sure needed some. The path this book put me on started a turnaround that continued until I finally recovered.

After reading "Peace Of Mind", I followed my practice of reading or re–reading other similar books, like "The Power Of Positive Thinking", by Norman Vincent Peale, and "How To Win Friends And Influence People", by Dale

Carnegie. Then I put that together with my training and experience to create my own way of doing it.

The Way You Think Makes Things Happen

"Positive mental attitude" has been used in business for motivating salespeople, for "visualization", used by athletes, and in many other ways that recognize the influence of positive and negative trains of thought on what actually happens in our lives.

All the writers said that thinking either positively or negatively causes different things to "happen" to you, and that you can have some control of what happens by paying attention to, and adjusting how much positive and negative is in your thinking.

It's Not What You Think It Is

Many people mistakenly think "positive attitude" means faking it. That you pretend things are good when they're not. They think it's about fooling yourself and others. This is not true, and is one reason I don't like the term, "positive attitude". It's not about those things at all, but is *a way of using a mechanism in your mind to your advantage*.

How Our Minds Work—Mental "Mo"

Like the writers above I found out for myself that there's a mechanism in our minds that makes us think and feel more and more the way we are already thinking and feeling. Simple, but powerful! Our thoughts and feelings are multiplied, extended, and sustained, whether they are positive or negative. Call it a kind of mental **"mo", or momentum**. What we are thinking and feeling, we go on thinking and feeling, *and these thoughts and feelings actually cause things to happen.*

In other words, mostly negative thoughts and attitudes *make negative things happen*, and mostly positive thoughts and attitudes *make positive things happen.*

And it just so happens that people suffering from PTSD and depression have mostly negative thoughts and attitudes! Aha!

To understand and use this mind trick can bring major changes for the better. Not only can it affect how we think and feel, *it can actually change what happens to us!* We do this by learning how to control and choose the direction of our mental "mo"—we learn to change the negative into the more positive.

Real Life Examples

For example, have you noticed how someone who whines and complains affects our feelings and thoughts? They make us uncomfortable, and we feel worse after talking with them than before. We can't wait to get away from them. Afterward, we may not be able to get the bad thoughts out of our head, and may think of even more bad things. By contrast, have you ever been caught up in the good feeling that being with a really positive person can bring? Suddenly, we're having fun, and our mood soars upward. We forget our cares for a while. We like being around these people, because they make us feel good.

It's as though these people are infectious, but each brings a very different kind of "infection". Well, it doesn't stop there. *You can actually "infect" yourself* with thoughts of your own choosing, creating positive "mo" or negative "mo". That's how it worked for me.

The mind doesn't care which it is. It just puts out more of whatever you put in. But believe me, it matters a great deal to us whether what we put in is positive or negative. It can be the difference between happiness or unhappiness, joy or sadness, maybe even life or death. So it pays to learn how to use this powerful tool.

A Secret: Just A Little More Positive Than Negative

The big secret: For this to work, I learned through trial and error that all you have to do is *make your thoughts a **little bit** more positive than negative*, and it will tip your mind like a see–saw into positive territory.

Would it surprise you to learn that victims of child abuse tend to average more negative thoughts and feelings than positive? C'mon, you know that already. Depression and PTSD are by definition massive negativity, and when you have them, they tend to spiral downward into even greater negativity. And a bad self–image is a self–perpetu-ating thing. All these things tend to drag you down, and make you feel worse and worse.

Once I learned how to create a more positive pattern of thinking, my feelings were more pleasant, more often.

And there was now a floor under my depression—the spiral would go so low, and no lower. This just happened, all by itself, once I got into more positive thinking territory. And the amount of time in depression declined, all without any medication or therapy. It wasn't a cure, and there was much more to do, but I was in much better shape to go forward. Now let's look at how it worked for me.

What I *Didn't* Have To Do

I didn't have to be positive all the time to make it work. And I didn't pretend, or deny when things really were bad, or when I felt bad. It's not a "put on a happy face" thing. Instead, using certain techniques that I will describe, I just learned to make my thinking and attitudes more positive, on the average. Again, it worked like a scale, or a see–saw.

All you have to do is tip it over a little to the positive side, and it falls all the way in that direction. That means that, while there still may be plenty of negative in your thinking and attitudes, the total picture only needs to be a little more positive than negative, in order to gain a benefit. That doesn't sound hard, and it isn't.

Why does this work? Got me. It's just the way our minds work. For me, positive thoughts and attitudes bring more positive thoughts and feelings, and even make more positive things happen. Which is what you want. On the other hand, negative brings more negative, including negative events. Which is already your problem, and not what you want. You can prove this to yourself.

How I Do It

As always, the first step is *noticing* what your thoughts and attitudes are. Simply pay attention to what you are thinking and feeling. You can write it down if that helps. Also notice the thoughts and attitudes of the other people in your life, because they do influence your thinking. As you become more aware, you will eventually have to ask yourself if you're living in a negative environment, and take steps to get away from negative influences.

Plus, *you probably have been creating your own negative self–environment*. Most child abuse victims will find that they do have a significant amount of negative thinking and attitudes, because that's what happens when you're abused. Left unchecked, these attitudes will actually attract bad things your way, and will create circumstances for more bad things to happen. You can probably think of some ways this has already happened.

Say you make a mistake. You may then catch yourself thinking: *"You stupid @*(*!" Or, "Why did I DO that?!" "I'm a miserable %$@(*!"* Beat self, beat self, beat self. Now, how does this help you correct the error? What does it make you feel about yourself? When you catch this, you can think, "Wait a minute. I just made a mistake. No big deal. I'll figure out how to fix it now." And, "We all make mistakes. It's wrong to beat myself up over it." What does thinking **that** make you feel?

Or say you're hanging out with a neighbor, who's doing a monologue on how bad he feels, how rotten everybody is, and how lousy the world is in general. Ugh. We know how that feels. All you can think is: "Let me out of here!" Well, who says you have to stay? You can suddenly remember something important you have to do, and escape with a smile. Afterward, you may have to do something to get back in a positive frame of mind.

Or look at the other side of the coin. You start off the day feeling good. You then wind up accomplishing a lot. Your boss praises you for good work. You're on a roll, so you spend a happy evening with your best pal, and feel like it's been one of the best days ever. One good thing led to another, and that's how positive "mo" works.

So for me, changing to a more positive attitude is a **method** for making more good things happen in your life, and for giving you more strength and confidence, and the power to direct your future. Now let's see what some of these techniques are.

Pay Attention To Your Thoughts

As I said, the first technique is to pay attention to your thoughts, and to the behavior of the other people in your life. Then, every time you catch yourself in negativity, think: "STOP!" Say: "This is a negative thought or attitude, and it's not helping me one bit. If there is a real problem, I need to think, then take positive action to solve it. But I will not dwell in negativity for its own sake". Next, replace the negative thought or attitude with a positive one that is realistic and true in that situation. I did that a lot.

For example, say that a stranger has said something nasty to you out of the blue, and they are no longer there.

You are taken by surprise, and start to get angry. You begin to think of good comebacks, and are feeling worse by the minute. Suddenly you realize your negative train of thought, and what it's doing to you. You realize that the stranger has no meaning to you, and it is not a problem to be solved. You tell yourself, "Stop!"

You may realize that it's the stranger's problem, having to live with his own nastiness and the bad things it brings. You replace your train of thought with a pleasant one, like what a nice day it is, or something good that's coming up. You can distract yourself in many ways—whatever works for you.

Projecting Love

A technique I've tried in this situation is to project love/pity (or compassion) toward the offender. A key thing was to realize that I didn't deserve it, and it was them, not me, who should be ashamed. Abuse victims tend to believe they somehow caused or deserved such a thing, and that can cause intense anger, and even trigger PTSD. We have to learn to get over this false perception of always being the one at fault. And to do that, we have to see clearly that it *is* false.

When you do these things, and keep doing them, you are re–training your mind, and after a while, you will naturally think more positively. Remember, the goal is slightly more positive thinking than negative, not positive perfection! You just want to tip the scales over to the plus side.

The Rubber Band Technique

Another technique I used is to wear a rubber band on my wrist. Every time I caught myself in useless negativity, I snapped the rubber band on my wrist. The slight pain I felt helped me to stop the negativity. I found this really worked well for me, especially at first.

Notice The Good Things

Another thing I've done is to notice and emphasize the positive. When a good thing is true, say it to yourself, or say it out loud if appropriate. If it's a nice day, stop, take a deep breath, and say: *"What a beautiful day!"* If someone is nice to you, say: *"What a nice/sweet person!"* If you've been thinking, *"I can't",* think, *"I can!"* If you've thought *"I'll never"*, think, *"I will!"* If you've been focusing on something bad around you for a little too long, look around for something good, and focus on that. Then ***notice how it makes you feel when you do this***. If you're alone somewhere, take a deep breath, smile big, and say out loud: *"***I feel GREAT!***"*

Notice how that makes you feel. Look in the mirror in the morning, smile and bellow: *"It's going to be a **great** day!"* These are ways to start positive trains of thought, and they really make you feel better. And they raise the odds that better things will happen. One reason: When you are in a good mood, you are more likely to recognize and act on good opportunities than when you are upset and unhappy. When you're deep in negativity, you won't even notice an opportunity, and so it passes you by. It kind of works like this: Positive thoughts > Positive feelings > Positive actions > Positive results (the same is true for negative thoughts). I still do this, and it makes life better.

Positive Imaging

Another technique is sometimes called imaging, or visualization. *What you see in your mind, you tend to find ways to make happen.* If those pictures are bad things, well, then you will tend to make bad things happen. If they are your heart's desires, and your biggest goals, then your mind will work to make *them* happen. Doing this somehow pulls things together in your mind and body to help produce the desired result.

The Subconscious Mind

Some say that the subconscious mind is the power behind this, and I think that's probably true. Feed it positive suggestions, and it works to make them come true. Suddenly you have a "eureka" moment, and know the next thing you must do. What happens here is that, fed positive suggestions, your subconscious mind keeps aware of them under the surface. It keeps turning over your goals and problems, looking for solutions and ways around obstacles. Then an idea for a solution may seem to just "pop up" in your conscious mind. This often happens when you "sleep on it".

And when there is an opportunity related to one of your goals, the subconscious mind will recognize it, and you will suddenly "see" an opportunity. With no goals or positive suggestions in the mind, these opportunities are likely to pass unnoticed, and you "miss" the opportunity.

We Can Make Our Dreams Come True

However this mechanism works, it's real. Athletes call it "visualization", and picture the outcome they want, down to the smallest movements. They swear it helps their performance. People dream dreams, and picture them happening, and then they happen.

How One Person Did It

In the late 1800's, a young black girl on a dirt-poor South Carolina farm, one of 15 children, dreamed of getting a college education. Her dream infected others, and somehow, she got that education,because they helped her. Then, with virtually no money, she went to Daytona Beach, Florida, dreaming of "buildings and students". She infected others with her dream, and started a small girl's school in a few tumbledown old cabins. She baked pies to sell for her school, and with the help of others, the school grew.

The young woman's name was Mary Bethune, co–founder of Bethune–Cookman University (Mr. Cookman was someone with money she convinced to help her). She not only got to see her "buildings and students" become real, but became a close friend of Eleanor Roosevelt, and was part of the Roosevelt Administration. And she was, and still is, an inspiration for many others. Not bad for a poor southern black farm girl in the days before integration!

And it happened because she kept picturing her dreams happening. Then she acted on them.

It Will Change Your Life

That is what more positive thinking and attitudes can do for anyone. All we have to do is harness it, and use it. This can change a person's life, even your life. It changed mine.

Look At Your Social Environment

An obvious thing to do is to pay attention to the thoughts and attitudes of the people you associate with. No more pity parties or gloom and doom conventions. If you find that some of your associates are constantly negative, *spend less time with them.*

Maybe you were doing a lot of the negativity, so first try changing the subject. Many "friendships" are based on griping and complaining, and that is not good for you.

If you've been watching a lot of negative TV programs, stop. Some of the worst are local news programs that feature non-stop worry points, crime and sex offenses. Always delivered with a frown, and with cooked-up anxiety in the voice. They blow these things way out of proportion to hook chronic worriers, and get more ratings. Also there are the national networks, cable news and radio *"unhappy-talk"* shows that elevate sarcastic griping and gossip to the highest levels, and (on the "news" channels) feature endless heated arguments about anything and everything, usually "much ado about *nothing*"! These things affect us all in a bad way, and especially those who are already saturated with negativity. Look at all aspects of your environment, and root out as much background negativity as you can. You'll be surprised how much better you will feel, right away.

Affirmations

Another technique a therapist taught me I'll call "affirmation". That is a true positive statement that you write down and say many times a day. Often these affirmations will be counter–statements to the bad things that were said about you when you were being abused. Or they can counter any negative thinking that you find is keeping you down. Here are a few of my own examples:

I am a good person.

Many people like who I am.

You can't please everyone.

I do my best most of the time, and my best is good enough.

My life is getting better now. I am learning to be more myself.

I will do whatever I have to do to become what I want to be.

I find a way to enjoy every day.

I'm glad to be alive right now.

There are good things in my future.

I can make good things happen that I want.

I notice and enjoy all the good things in my life, and am thankful for them.

You get the idea. I found if you say these things long enough and often enough, that is how you will begin to think (when underlying negative feelings are resolved). You were taught to think bad things, and you can learn to think good things, instead. And when you think more good thoughts, you will have more good feelings. And your life will change for the better.

It Works!

It did for me. Besides getting that floor under my depression, good things started to happen, because I was making them happen. For several years, we'd had no hope of ever owning our own home, but within eight short months of my learning this method, we moved in! I still had a long way to go, but this knowledge of positive thinking and attitudes was like a life preserver. It got me moving in the right direction, and set the stage for more good things to come. That makes it *one of the key factors* in my healing and recovery.

Yoga, Meditation, Relaxation, and The Like

The above ways of calming the mind and body, along with some others can be very helpful for dealing with anxiety and other mind and body (psychosomatic) problems. These are positive things you can do. Physical relaxation techniques, along with yoga postures, Tai Chi Chuan movements, Mindfulness, Pilates, etc. can provide physical release of tension, and some mental relief. So can walking, bicycling, and other forms of exercise. I've found that *exercise is a key* for reducing tension and anxiety. It can pay to try some of these things to see what helps.

What Is Meditation?

What I most want to tell you is what I learned about meditation, that I haven't seen mentioned much.

I always thought meditation meant saying a *"mantra"* over and over, so that your mind becomes focused and gradually less distracted. But the surprise I found is that *there are many, many forms of meditation*, sometimes things that you don't think of as meditation. Let me explain: *Meditation is ANY way of focusing your mind.* It can be a sound, a thought, a sensual feeling, such as wind on your skin, a sight, such as raindrops sliding down a window, a burning candle, or even focusing on parts of your body as you relax them. Anything that brings you into the present moment and disconnects you from the thought stream running through your head works. Most meditations that help tend to evoke what's been called the "relaxation response", as opposed to the "stress response".

What this means is there is some kind of meditation you can find that will work for you. My favorites these days are:

1) (and for me by far the most effective) *Mindfulness*,

where you focus sensually on the present moment. You also learn how to handle the distracting thought stream, and to embrace it as natural. A main form of mindfulness involves focusing on the breath.

2) ***Soothing sounds and places***, like ocean or river waves, nature sounds, some new age, classical, or other music. I keep looking for new kinds, as certain ones better fit certain situations than others. I'm finding it's possible to meditate several different ways, many times a day.

That's really good because yoga and meditation are proven to help calm nerves, lower blood pressure, and slow the heartbeat, among other things. I recommend you look into it. I'm really very impressed with *mindfulness* as taught by Dr. Jon Kabat–Zinn, who has been teaching and practicing for a long time. I highly recommend his books, especially *"Full Catastrophe Living"*. He's very good at explaining things clearly, and shows how mindfulness as a way of life can improve your health and make you more whole. He's also very good at explaining Eastern ideas to the Western mind.

Next, we'll talk about some related topics: Finding and living your own life, and the power of goals.

Chapter Eighteen

Living Your Own Life

Trying to be someone else never works, because you can only be you! So why do so many child abuse victims keep trying to be someone else?

Trying To Live For Someone Else

We've already established that much of your behavior as a child was an attempt to please a parent who could never be pleased; that you were likely told over and over that you were no good the way you were, and that what you were was unacceptable; that your attempts to assert and be yourself were met with anything from ridicule to violence; that your every fault (real or imagined) was magnified into a fatal flaw; that your every mistake was noted as justification for cruelty and rejection; that your achievements were minimized, even made fun of.

And so you reject yourself, and strive to please others, and try to be what you think they want you to be. That's how it was for me.

The Carrot And The Stick

For the victim of abuse, parental "approval" and vicious punishment are the carrot and the stick that force you away from your own life and into one of confusion, frustration, and unhappiness. You may be a perfectionist, which hinders your progress. Or you may be a rebel, and are living to "prove" something.

It's Not Easy To Solve

This is an obstacle for abuse victims, based on intense fears and over-used defenses, resulting from years of abuse. The feelings that support your tendency to please others and not yourself are very strong, and hard to overcome. Recovery from this requires a lot of determined hard work, and some help. These forces want to turn you away from your natural path in life, and you have to find a way to stay on it.

But You Can Do It

When most people make decisions about who they are and what they want, they relax and rely on their feelings or "instincts". *Abuse victims can't do that*, because their "instincts" have been twisted as a result of the abuse. But there is a "real you" in there, and you can find it! For me, the trick was to learn to separate the *real me* from the *imposed "me"*. So you'll have to analyze which "instincts" are *"you"*, and which are *"not you"*.

Uncovering The "Not You"

Here are some clues that helped me uncover the "not you":

Things that convince you that you shouldn't do what you really want because

- *There isn't enough money in it*

- *It's not "practical"—can't do that*

- *It's not what I **should** do*

- *It's not what everyone **expects** of me*

- *It's too much trouble for those around me*

- *I could never do it anyway, it's too hard*

- *It will cost too much*

- *It's just a pipe dream*

- *I don't deserve it*

- *It doesn't matter what I do, I can learn to like anything*

- *I'm being too selfish by wanting that*

These are all poor excuses for not being you, and if you follow them, you'll be sorry later. What you do as your life's work *does* matter. You're made the way you are, and that "you" is meant to do certain things. You are a unique person with unique desires, talents and ambitions, and neither you or those around you will be as happy if you give up on your dreams, and give up on being yourself.

"Good" Reasons—Not!

Other people may give you "good reasons" why you shouldn't do what you really want. Some will tell you that *you don't have the talent, you'll never make it, it's silly or impossible, etc.* A lot of very happy and successful people ignored such advice, and proved the nay–sayers wrong, and we've all heard these stories. The whole point of being yourself is to *not* listen to what others say when they try to discourage you from doing what you want. This is one thing where *you're the expert*! No one else can tell you what you really want. And only you can figure out if you have what's needed to get what you want, or if you can acquire it. Just know that there is a way to be yourself in your work, and in the way you live your life, and that you can find it.

A Waste

Remember that life spent trying to be someone else is life *wasted*. And when you set out on the wrong path, it will take you farther and farther away from the right one, and make it harder and harder to get back on track.

A Self Inventory

To solve this problem you can take an inventory of who you really are, and of the reasons and ways that you try to be someone you aren't. I did all these things:

- What do you enjoy doing in your free time? Rate your daily activities by the level of enjoyment they bring.

- What kind of person are you? Outgoing or introvert; outdoorsy or city lover; intellectual or laid back. Reader? Like travel? In what settings are you consistently happy? Make a profile of yourself.

- Keep a "my way" notebook, where you write down all the ideas you get on the subject, and review and add to them daily. Focusing in this way will give you new ideas and approaches for living the life you want. This is a good way to use the positive mental "mo" we talked about to create a positive change. And it's fun to think about this!

- Take an "interest inventory" test at a local college or community college. They can help you learn about your unique combo of interests.

- Ask what work you would do if you had all the money you needed. What would be your priorities? Is there a way to work more of this ideal scenario into your life now?

- List all your daily activities, plus ones you want to try. Mark down the level of satisfaction (1 to 10) you *think* each one will give you, *before* you do it.

- Then, after you've done it, mark down the level of satisfaction it *actually* provided. Sometimes, the before and after levels will be surprisingly different! This can tell you something.

It's important for you to do these exercises, as you were trained not to know these things. Don't feel bad about not knowing, just find out, and act on what you learn. Then inventory the reasons why you try to be someone else. The clearer you get on this, the less power your past will have over you.

Being told you're no good the way you are is a common reason for this, and wanting your parent's approval (we all do) is another.

Let's make one thing clear. Will everyone be able to fulfill their *exact* dream? Maybe, maybe not. If you always wanted to be a professional football lineman, and you weigh 135 lbs. soaking wet, it's not going to happen. But you could be a sportswriter or cameraman. You could learn the game and coach. If you love football, you can be involved with it somehow. There is always a way to be who you are, that will satisfy. You just have to look for, and find it.

Who am I *not*?

You can make a list of the things that you are *"supposed to" be*, and that are *not* you. Aside from having good manners, civil behavior, and basic consideration of others, we can be *anything else we want!* Keep this list around to remind you where you *don't* want to go.

You have a right to be who you really are, the person you were born to be. And to try to do what you want with your life. We all do. What you are is just fine—***you don't need permission***.

Of course, it won't be easy. You'll be tempted to give up and go back to more "comfortable", familiar, dead–end ways. Just keep on heading your own way, and you'll know the happiness of being yourself!

Once you're going in the right direction, you'll need to know how to set and achieve goals, which is our next topic.

Chapter Nineteen

The Power Of Goals

There's a book title that *perfectly* describes why we need goals: *"If You Don't Know Where You're Going, You'll Probably End Up Somewhere Else,"* by David Campbell, Ave Maria Press, 2005.

Life With And Without A Road Map

Without goals, we're like objects floating on a gigantic sea, bobbing along to anywhere and nowhere. My first contact with goals came at an outfit called the Jaycees, or Junior Chambers of Commerce. They taught us that *with* goals, a determined person will achieve much or most (if not all) of what they seek. But without them, achievement is unlikely.

Planning For A Step At A Time

To make goals takes a lot of thought. You need to know exactly what you're aiming for. To do that, you need to know yourself, and what your priorities are. Then you have to break down the main goal into in–between goals, each one a small step in your march toward your desired end.

There's an old saying' *"the longest journey begins with one small step"*. Achieving a goal requires dozens, perhaps hundreds of small steps. In fact, *a key to success is the smallness of each step*. What can be overwhelming when viewed all at once can be easy when viewed little piece by little piece.

Having goals and working on them brings hope and excitement to your life, especially when they come from your heartfelt dreams and desires. And they can bring more order and control to a chaotic life.

Especially Important To Abuse Victims

Abuse victims have ***built–in success–stoppers***. It's very, very hard to achieve, or even sustain an effort when you are totally focused on just surviving. Depression and PTSD can steal all your time and energy. In these circumstances, basic functioning and survival are achievements to be proud of.

But, of course, we all want a lot more than just survival. And that's where the tool of goal setting comes in. It's a method for rising above survival mode, and for propelling yourself toward your dreams, even while still fighting the results of abuse. It's a tool for getting your life back.

What Goals Should You Have?

The *first* thing to do is to spend time deciding what your goals will be. That requires solving the problems of the last chapter, "Finding And Living Your Own Life". You'll have to learn to separate the "not you" from the "real you", or you'll wind up with goals that take you just where you *don't* want to go. Ideally, your goals will be based solidly on who you are, and will lead you to just the life you would like to live.

For example, I'm a person who is deliriously happy when outdoors in nature, and especially when seeing a park or hiking trail for the first time. I also like to write. So guess what one of my goals could be? Traveling nature writer! I didn't have to be a genius to figure that out, but I did have to take the time to analyze myself and think of ways that would satisfy my personal desires. And I have to figure out a practical way to do the traveling nature writing (this book has to be done first, something I also want).

It's About What You Enjoy

While "what you're good at" plays a role in your decisions, *it's not necessarily the key factor*. I'm also good at social work and computer programming, but am not happy doing those things. So I didn't set my goals by saying: "I should be a social worker or programmer, because social work is noble, or because programming makes good money". It's not about money or nobility, but about what you *enjoy*.

Usually, both adequate money and respect will come when you follow your heart. That's because the person with a *passion* for what they do usually rises to the top of their profession. In fact, you may be able to invent a new kind of job to practice your heart's desire for work. It happens all the time—the internet, for example. Someone once said: "Do what you love and you'll never have to "work" a day in your life!" Not that all work is wonderful, even when you like it. You may not be able to quit your day job right away, but you can plan how to get from here to a better place.

A Focus For Our Thinking And Actions

What goals do is focus our thinking and actions on a specific desired result. And that brings positive mental "mo" into play. We're creating a positive train of thought that will take us where we want to go. The more we think about our goal, and *visualize* its fulfillment, the more excited we get. And the more ideas pop into our heads for what we can do to get there.

And the more we recognize opportunities to get there when they come along (instead of sleeping through them). We become a rolling freight train on a track to somewhere! It makes life worth living, and brings a kind of happiness you can get no other way.

Different Kinds Of Goals

There are several different kinds of goals we can use on our journey to somewhere. Basically, they are *short–term goals*, and *long–term goals*. And these can further break down into hourly, daily, weekly, monthly, quarterly, yearly, five–year, ten–year, etc. goals. Each one requires thinking and planning.

For example, a daily goal for my "traveling nature writer" super-goal might be to do one thing each day from a list of research, observation, or writing. A weekly goal might be to study successful similar writing by others. A monthly goal might be to assess progress toward a completed article. An initial yearly goal might be to produce 4 articles. And so on.

The more detailed, accurate and practical your goals are, the clearer you can visualize the main goal being reached. And *when you can visualize in sharp detail, you are more likely to achieve the goal*. This comes with practice, and you will definitely adjust and change your goals with experience.

Not Giving Up

It's one thing to adjust your goal to a practical reality. It's another thing entirely to say: "My goal isn't practical, so I'll just have to give up". When we haven't been down a path before, we don't know what we'll find. It's likely there will be obstacles, wrong turns, failures, mistakes and disappointments. Those things are a given in all human endeavors.

We may decide to make some sensible changes to our goals, based on experience. We may even *change our mind* about a goal, and decide for really good reasons not to pursue it further. But we should *never* give up on ourselves, or on our dreams. They are our hopes for joy and happiness and fulfillment, and what's life without that?

We need to be flexible enough to know when to take a different path, or pursue a different goal, but we should be stubborn about where we're heading, and that it's really where we want to go. Then, while we may not achieve 100% of our goal, we will get a good part of it.

So sit down and work out your own goals, to meet your own needs and desires. Break them down into small pieces you can handle, and begin your own march toward fulfillment.

My book title would say: *"If You Know Where You're Going, Keep Your Eye On Your Goals, Break Them Down Into Manageable Pieces, And Don't Give Up. Then You'll Probably Wind Up Where You Want To Be"*!

Use this method and you'll outmaneuver bad luck, overcome setbacks, and get where you want to be. Good luck!

That concludes the section on tools for recovery. Next we'll talk about the relationships in your life, including the question of whether you can forgive your abusing parent(s).

Part Five

The Relationships
In Your Life

Here we'll talk about the important people in your life: Your spouse, children, friends and co-workers. And yes, your abuser, too.

There were things I had to realize about how I affected my spouse and children. And there were things we all learned so that my suffering did not have to extend a great deal into their lives as well.

I had to find a new relationship with my parents, and deal with questions of guilt and other negative emotions, and of forgiveness.

Chapter Twenty

Issues That Affect Relationships

Everyone has problems in their relationships. But child abuse victims have special ones that are the result of their abuse. And the sooner we learn how to handle them, the better our relationships will work out.

In this chapter I'll tell about how I improved my relationships.

First I want to talk about general things: Denial and other defensive problems; trust; fear; anger; and shame. Then we'll look at relationships with those closest to us, and how we can improve those relationships.

General Problems With Other People

Denial

We've talked about this already, but it's also a problem for relationships.

As I've said, denial can lock us into never-ending cycles of mistrust, fear, anger and depression, and blaming others. And it can keep us from making any progress at all. We may be extremely afraid of truths that are the only way to freedom, where the truth is actually not as bad as we fear.

It Affects Relationships

Besides holding back recovery, denial and other defenses (projection, etc.) can hurt or destroy relationships. People will get tired or frustrated when you repeatedly sidestep reality. And they can be hurt or even shocked when you blame them for your problems.

That's because they are living in the real world, and you aren't. Especially frustrating to you and them is when you feel better, and announce it's all O.K. now. Then it all happens again—an "Oh, No!" moment.

The only real solution is to find a good therapist who can help you get past your toxic defenses. And to stop denying.

Super Big Warning!

If you listen to anything I'm saying, listen to this: I want to strongly WARN YOU AGAIN that messing with your defenses by yourself is dangerous! While the defenses may be faulty, they usually keep us from reaching the breaking point, which could happen if you try to remove them by yourself. We're after better health here, not a nervous breakdown. As they say, ***don't try this at home! Find and use a good therapist.***

Oh, No!

Cycles of depression and PTSD, followed by calm periods, can help keep toxic defenses going. You can get a false belief that when you feel better for a while, the problems are gone for good. But these problems won't go away by themselves—you have to **DO** things to make them go away. So the short–lived happiness is crushed when the problems come back. And, like me, each time that happens, you can lose a little more hope, and your spirit can be crushed a little more. If you don't face the problems, they will get worse.

Until you see depression and PTSD as problems that are logical for you to have, and that you can solve, the hopeless cycle will continue. If denial or other defenses are an enemy of your recovery, get help to conquer that enemy!

Trust

If you were hurt and betrayed by the very person(s) in the world whose job it was to love and nurture you, you'll have problems trusting people. Trust comes from the love and nurture of early childhood. If you didn't get that, it's hard to trust.

Also, later stages of development are built on a basis of trust, so this can create what you could call "emotional growth or maturity gaps" as we grow older. Strong issues of mistrust can foster paranoia, jealousy, and fears of abandonment and rejection.

The Damage Need Not Be Permanent

I experienced most of those things at one time or another, but have few problems with them now. I was able to learn to trust more, love and nurture, and grow out of these issues. It helped a lot to have a loving wife who was raised the right way, and from whom I could learn. The fact that I could do this shows that much of the damage from abuse need not be permanent, and that it can be overcome. I think the main thing is to be open to changing these feelings, and to be willing to learn from others.

Depression will exaggerate mistrust and the feelings it causes. The effect of depression on this and other relationship problems makes it important to try to get help (if medically advised for you), in the form of an anti–depressant. An anti–depressant that works can make everything else you have to do easier. In my case, I was never able to make good progress until I found an effective anti–depressant.

Each Step Forward Makes You Stronger

Being in PTSD can make you appear to be delusional, or irrational about these issues, especially with paranoia, jealousy, fears and anger. That's no surprise, because PTSD puts you, emotionally, into a past bad reality. It's not exactly delusional, but more of a confusion between past and present, which is a hard thing to handle until you learn how. Because it happens out of the blue in response to a "trigger", there's a shock or upset factor, too.

What happened with me was that *each advance in any area* (medication, understanding, experience, help and learning) *made it easier to deal with everything else.* Every step forward for one problem added to strength and success in dealing with all other problems.

Fears

Being overly fearful can harm your relationships. When you're overly afraid, it changes your whole attitude and approach to life. And strong fears are a logical result of abuse. In fact, we're built to program fears into our brains in response to danger, pain, etc. This is a hard–wired survival trait. But abuse victims get overloaded with threat and danger messages, and with expectation of pain.

We *learn* fears to protect ourselves, and we can also *unlearn* them to some extent if we want to (Cognitive Behavioral therapy helps with this). Unlearning fears usually involves facing each one of them honestly, until we truly understand them and where they come from. It also involves *doing* the things we fear—standing up when your knees want to buckle. Or to put it another way, not avoiding things that scare you.

Anger

The anger from abuse is more like an underlying rage, which is what people feel when they are abused, and are unable to escape it. But since it's not safe to show anger to a parent that you feel is looking for an excuse to kill you, the anger gets buried in the unconscious mind. It later winds up fueling inappropriate anger responses to everyday frustrations and disappointments. You can appear to be much angrier than is normal at times, and may "lose your temper" over things that are associated in your mind with the abuse, whether they make sense in the present or not.

Of course this kind of thing can really mess up relationships with others, who don't understand where it's all coming from. They don't understand because they weren't abused, and don't have these buried feelings. Once you understand it, you'll need to explain it *only* to those who *must* know (mostly your spouse). It's not the kind of thing you can share with an employer or a casual friend or acquaintance. In many cases you'll just have to learn how to control these feelings around those who don't need to know. As you go forward with your recovery, there will be less to control.

When I came to understand my anger, and safely felt it full force, this problem kept getting smaller and smaller. Making that connection will require help.

Guilt And Shame

There's one more issue I'll call *"Guilt and shame"* due to having PTSD and depression. When you are in PTSD, you are overcome with the feeling that someone in the present has taken the role of your abuser. That could be your spouse or child, or an authority such as a boss. You may lash out, and say or do bad things, because you feel compelled to defend yourself in this way. Then, when you return to normal, you may feel guilt and/or shame for what you've said or done.

This is not exactly an ego or confidence builder. There are real things you may have said or done to feel guilty about, or ashamed of. To recover from this requires four things: Self–acceptance, self–forgiveness, and a sincere apology. And it requires your best efforts to gain control over your PTSD and your feelings. The more you recover, the less a problem this will be. Guilt and shame become pride in your recovery.

Accepting What Happened—It Wasn't Your Fault

Let's assume you're trying your best to recover. Now remember, you didn't ask to have these problems, they were given to you. While you are fully responsible for what you do, beating yourself over the head will not help you to change it. There should be no guilt or shame for *having* PTSD, which is something that was done to you. It's something you have to accept, and go from there. You also have the right to forgive yourself, as long as you are truly doing your best to overcome the problem. You must learn to be kind to yourself before you can truly be kind to others. An apology to one whose feelings you've hurt can be part of that kindness, and is also part of your own healing.

O.K, let's talk about how childhood abuse affects love relationships, and the love between husband and wife.

Love Relationships Of An Abuse Survivor

This area can be a minefield. So many things that result from abuse can make your love life painful and difficult. But like a minefield, these things can be de–fused, and made safe.

If the abuser was of the opposite sex, you are likely to be *both needy of and afraid of* persons of that sex. This can lead to stormy relationships, sex addiction, doubts about your sexuality, and having relationships for the wrong reasons or with the wrong person, to name only a few perils.

If the abuser was of the same sex, you will be ill–prepared for your normal roles in life, such as marriage, parenthood, and just feeling comfortable in your own skin. That's because we learn these things from our same–sex parent. You are likely to look to the outside world for clues, and you may get some really bad guidance that way. Or, you may get lucky like I did and find just the right person to go through life with.

Knowledge Sets You Free

One thing is true: *The more you understand about your needs and feelings, the better off you will be*. Without this knowledge, you may feel that you're stumbling around in the dark. Learning about yourself makes it possible for you to find real ways to handle these problems, and increases your odds of having a happy, successful life. This learning is a big part of recovery.

The Marriage Of An Abuse Survivor

It's easy to see that the burdens on a marriage when one partner was abused as a child can be great. It's hard enough to make a marriage work without such problems. And the jealousy, paranoia, fear, anger, depression and PTSD that you may bring to the table doesn't help.

Clearly, success will require a strong commitment from both spouses, and strong love between them. It will also require hard work, loyalty, faith, and other strong character traits in both people. What I know is that, if there is strong love, it can work out.

In order to get through what can be years of effort to reach recovery, the person who marries an abuse survivor will need a big heart, and an open, understanding mind. For the marriage to last, the spouse will need to go in feeling that the abuse victim's good points outweigh the difficulties involved. They'll have to really love them. And you'll have to make it clear you are trying your best to recover. Again the good news: It can happen, and happiness is possible.

I know that because, by some miracle, that's exactly the kind of woman I married. So over 49 years later, we're still at it. Looking back, we don't think much about the hard times, but mostly remember the good times, which have been many. And we both have no doubt it was all worth it. I think my good marriage was a key factor in my recovery, if not *the* key factor, and that getting this part of life right is worth whatever effort it takes.

Communicating

One key to a good marriage is good communication, which we know is about mutual listening. The feelings an abuse survivor has can be intense and disruptive to family life. So it's very important to have ways of sharing and defusing those feelings. And since the spouse will have their own feelings to deal with, communication must be a two way street.

You have to get to the point where you can both share your deepest feelings, knowing that the other will listen and look out for you. This is not something we're born knowing how to do. The techniques I described earlier, and perhaps counseling (family therapy) whenever a snag is reached, will help, and will increase your intimacy and the joy in your relationship.

Things A Spouse Can Do

It's important that the spouse of the abuse survivor tries to give unconditional love and acceptance, which is exactly what the abused never had as a child. Such acceptance is a powerful tonic for the abused. It is what they need and crave most. For this they will be very grateful, and what is given will be returned many times over.

If the sufferer has depression and PTSD, the spouse needs to learn how these things work, and what exactly are the triggers that set it off, so they can avoid them, and the resultant pain. Both the sufferer and the spouse need to know that the spouse cannot understand at first, because it is outside their own life experience. When the problems are shared and understood, you can find ways to solve them. There are more suggestions for the spouse in the chapter on PTSD, and in the next chapter.

With sincere effort and real love, abuse victims and their spouses can have all the joys in their marriage that anyone else can have. More self–knowledge and good communication can lead to a great life. Now, what about the children?

The Children Of The Abused—Loving And Protecting Them

We know what can happen if an adult child of abuse does *not* deal with the problems of their abuse. They will probably be abusive to their own children, passing the pain and suffering to the next generation. That's the best reason to do something about it. And be warned: *No matter how hard you try not to, you will probably hurt your children someday, somehow, because of your condition.* That is one of the awful legacies of being abused as a child.

I had a fierce determination that I would never hurt my children the way I was hurt. And the few times I slipped and said or did something bad were devastating to me. Thank goodness I was able to recover, and we all seem to have come through O.K.

Fortunately, the pain and damage can be minimal, and not life changing. You can reach the point where you know you've mostly spared your children from your fate. One of the great joys and achievements of fighting the good fight is to see one day that your children are happy and do not have the problems that you had.

The hardest problem to deal with is PTSD or deep depression, where you can temporarily lose control. Bad things can be said or done when you are in PTSD. What can you do?

First Put It In Perspective

If you somehow hurt your child, you may become overwhelmed by guilt and self–loathing, which will probably make things worse. Part of the problem with PTSD and depression is self–hate and the belief that you are bad and deserved to be abused. If you hurt your child, it will reinforce and increase your bad feelings about yourself.

On the other hand, it really is bad to hurt your child, and you may have promised yourself you would never do that. It's still your responsibility to protect your child.

What can you do? *First*, if you are doing all you can to recover, you are also helping your child. *Second*, you must apologize *every* time you hurt your child as soon as you are able. *Another* thing you can do when you're able is to let them tell you how what you did or said made *them* feel, and how it has affected *their* life.

You may not be able to do this very well until you are more recovered, but you can try your best, and in this way show them that you love and respect them, and that their feelings are important.

You Aren't The Only Family With Problems

A true perspective means knowing that most families have problems with raising children at one time or another. No one and no family are perfect. That's not to deny that being abusive to your children, especially if it's frequent, can harm them. But you don't want to go to the other extreme, where you are overwhelmed with guilt and self–hate, either.

Know that if you are trying hard to recover, and are showing your child love and respect when you are *not* ill, things will probably work out O.K. Try to walk the fine line between full responsibility for your actions and excessive guilt and self–hate.

"Just Discipline"

A very difficult area of child rearing for sufferers of past child abuse is discipline. Properly taught, discipline leads to self–discipline in the child, which is the basis for success and achievement in life. But for someone with PTSD, discipline can equal abuse. I'll never forget my parents telling me that the incidents of bad abuse were "just discipline".

And I'll never forget what an old social work boss said when asked, "What does a child need most from a parent? She said: "***Love and discipline***". So "*just discipline*" isn't enough!

There are a couple of ways to avoid harming your children with "discipline" (as opposed to the real thing that comes with love). *First*, be aware that this could be a problem for you, and seek advice from highly trusted people (like your spouse) when you're not sure. *Second*, your spouse must stand up for the child if you get off track, and you need to accept their concern and input, not as an attack on you or an insult, but as an act of love for all of you.

Your Child Needs You Too

One warning here. It's important that the spouse not take over completely. In your family relationship the sufferer should not be labeled as "crazy", unreliable, or incompetent as a parent. Too much protectiveness by the spouse can lead to that, which is not good for the children. What that can do is turn the sufferer into a weak or absent parent, and the child needs *two* strong parents.

Remember, the sufferer is normal and competent when they are not in PTSD, except for certain ways they may be denying or defensive.

It can be a struggle sometimes to balance protection with good relationships, but you just have to try to do both.

They Know, But May Not Understand

Children are indeed vulnerable, but they can tell whether a parent loves them, and whether they are trying hard to be a good parent. At the same time, though, you have to realize **that *it is likely to be confusing to a child when their parent behaves in two different ways*** (ie: loving and angry). That's a hurdle you have to get over by letting them tell you how this two–sidedness makes them feel. To be a good parent, one thing you need to learn is how to communicate (listen) effectively with your child. And we all have different ways of doing that.

So with ground rules of what is out of bounds (being abusive), The spouse should try to encourage the sufferer to develop their own relationship with their child, in a way that works for the child and for the sufferer. ***And both parents have to address the two–sidedness of the suffering parent.*** That's what's best for the child.

Remember that a child finds his own identity through identifying with parent or parents, so not letting them have a real relationship with the sufferer will do their healthy development more harm than good. You only get one set of parents, so a decent relationship with a parent who has problems is much better than no relationship at all. And communication lines should be open whenever possible.

What About Real Danger To The Child?

Make no mistake. If there is a *real, present danger to the child*, the child must be protected, and nothing else matters more. If there has been sexual abuse or a beating, that is a crime, and the authorities should be involved.

For other things, it's not so simple. As a former child abuse and neglect worker, I know that the best thing doesn't always happen for the child when authorities become involved. Sometimes intervention is needed, sometimes it is not. Mistakes are sometimes made, and a mistake can have bad consequences for the child.

As a rule, the best place for a child who is *not* in danger is with their parents (possibly with helpers involved). As a caseworker, it seemed I always could tell if the child was really in danger, and in those cases I acted immediately. And for me, those cases were very few. Most often, the family needed help, and could stay together.

Therefore, *if, and only if, the child is* **not** *in danger*, but the situation is temporarily unmanageable, seek trusted outside help, I'd suggest in the form of family therapy. Some of the best family therapists are PhD psychologists and MSW social workers who specialize in this.

Here's how I would handle these questions:

Please keep in mind, these decisions are your responsibility, not mine.

If either the sufferer or the spouse believes there is real danger, *there is no choice*—you *must* contact the authorities **OR** a qualified therapist, who is bound by law (in most states—check yours) to decide if the authorities need to be notified. In other words, you may be able to let the therapist help you make that decision.

If the sufferer is working hard to recover and is reaching out to the child, and *no one* believes there is danger, I would just keep working on it.

If you come to a place where you have stopped making progress, I would ask my good helper to recommend a good family therapist. They are able to treat the family as a whole, and maintain the importance of each family member.

What Else Can You Do?

If you have sometimes hurt your child by what you have said or done, you can either help them with their resultant feelings, or have your family therapist do it with you, when the child is receptive to doing this.

If there has been hurt, the child will probably have some anger about your behavior, which can trigger more PTSD in you. So you'll have to be careful about how fast or far you go with this. *Never try to do it when in PTSD or depression.* If you can't do it, you should use a family therapist. And you can ask your own good therapist what they think you can and can't do. The more you have recovered, the more you should be able to tolerate the child's anger, if you have learned about your own hidden anger over how you were treated.

When In Doubt, Get Help

The goal is to be able to allow the child to feel and show that anger (or their confusion), and deal with it honestly, without triggering PTSD in you. This may not be possible for you to do alone. It's is easier to do with a trusted therapist than it is to do by yourself, because of your PTSD. You can find a way to avoid having your child hide their anger, like you had to. However you are able to handle it, just love the child with all your heart, *tell* them so, and *show* it in your actions. Keep trying your best, and it will work out. *Just don't deny if there's a problem that has to be addressed.*

You And Your Spouse Need To Work Together

If you have been fighting with your spouse over your relationships with your children, see if both of you can shift toward better communication. If your spouse stops you from hurting your child, *that is a good and necessary thing, but how they do it is also important*. As I've said, labeling you as a bad parent or "the wrong one', or 'the crazy one" is not a good thing for the child, who needs both parents to grow and thrive. It's right to protect the child, but not to exclude a parent, unless there is a real issue of safety.

Use good communication skills, and encourage your spouse to give support to your desire not to hurt the children, and to be part of their lives. Remember that a child needs a good relationship with both parents in order to grow into a healthy adult. That includes the parent who was abused as a child, and each parent has to form that relationship *in their own way*. For this to happen, the spouse will need to trust you. Discussions about this should never be attempted while you are in PTSD or depression.

In my case, I worked hard at *not* hurting my children, and am sure I failed a few times. There have been signs my problems disturbed them at times. One child said the two–sidedness was confusing. But they both know I love them, and neither has *my* problems, so I believe we have succeeded at protecting them from my heritage of abuse (thanks in great part to their wonderful mother).

And as I have healed and recovered, our relationships have become *really* good. To me, that has been a real blessing. Maybe it turned out that way because I so badly wanted it to.

I'll close this subject with *a few things one should **NOT** do to a child*:

- *Make them feel responsible for your pain, or your feelings in general.*
- *Be dependent on them.*
- *Foster unreasonable guilt.*
- *Make them feel bad about themselves.*
- *Blame them for your own problems or failures.*
- *Discourage their independence.*
- *Fail to respect their individuality.*
- *Fail to respect them as a person*
- *Fail to encourage them to live their own life.*

Children are one of the great joys of life. Enjoy them!

Finally, we'll talk about your relationships in the working world.

Handling The Working World

It's unfortunate, but the working world is not likely to react with warmth and understanding if you announce you have bad depression or PTSD. If your instinct is to keep it to yourself, *you are right*. Just don't avoid actually treating and taking care of it because of what "others might think".

Being Realistic

In my opinion, our world is barely past the stone age when it comes to people with problems like ours. Others may be into immortality or macho fantasies, and see you as weak. Or they may be afraid to get too close in case they might "catch" it. Expect it if your problem is obvious.

All this means is that some people are ignorant about your situation (they never experienced it), and that does not reflect on you. You don't have to waste time and energy being mad at them. A really strong person faces their problems and fears, and does something about it.

And a really strong person can put up with people who are shallow, immature, or simply unknowing. When you get done healing and recovering, you'll be a heck of a lot stronger than most people! And yes, there are plenty of folks with intelligence and good character, too (but don't expect that these will all understand either).

So you'll have to *be careful whom you share with*. As long as you can do the job well, and get along well enough with your co-workers, *who needs to know?* You are likely to have problems with negative or sadistic people, and you will have to work this out. Such people can trigger PTSD. And while you may be able to "swallow" your bad feelings, your body and feelings may be in an uproar.

I think that *if you are under a really bad supervisor, you may need to consider another job*. Otherwise you may develop psychological and psychosomatic problems.

A Better Chance For Success

It pays for people like us to do a few things to increase the odds of success.

- Train for the thing that you *really* enjoy doing, as opposed to the "practical" thing, or "sensible" thing. Loving what you do will get you past a lot.

- Get as much training and education as you can, so you have more choice of better jobs.

- If you are already doing something you *don't* like, work on changing to something you do like, and keep on until you get there.

- Pay attention to the job atmosphere, and to the personality of your supervisor when you interview for a job. *Avoid people who are obviously difficult like the plague*, which they are for you. The job that "feels" best may just be the best, even with lower pay.

- Consider jobs where you are independent, like having your own business or other enterprise. This can give you more "space" for healing and recovery, and you can be your own supervisor. Be warned, it's not the easy way.

Well, we've talked a lot about relationships, and I've told you about some of the things I've learned for myself over the years. Just know that having problems like ours doesn't mean you have to miss anything important in life, or that you can't have the good things. If you work at healing and recovery, you can have more than you may have ever thought possible. You can have good and rewarding relationships.

Years ago, I didn't think I'd have a very good life, and I was wrong. Good things may be waiting for you, if you just go for it and don't give up.

Now I'd like to speak to the loved ones of those who were abused, to see if I can help you also.

Chapter Twenty-One

For Those Who Love Us

The problems of an adult abuse victim are also problems for their family. But this can be handled. If there is love, things can be overcome. The best thing the survivor can do for everyone is to work steadily on their recovery. And the more the family can understand about the problem, the more they can help, and the less pain will be felt by all.

So this chapter is meant to help the family understand. I'll try to explain what the survivor is going through, and discuss positive things you can do. I assume that you love the abuse survivor, and would like to see them recover, and all of you want to be happier.

It's Not Your Fault, Either!

You have problems to handle that you may not have expected, and don't understand. If you didn't go through what the abuse survivor did, you really *won't* understand it, because it's outside your experience. You may find yourself feeling bad things, like guilt or shame, and may somehow feel responsible for your loved one's pain. Let's make one thing very clear. *You aren't responsible.* The abusing parents are the ones responsible for it.

Things You Can Do

So what can you do? First, what about you? You have feelings too, and so do your children. These feelings are just as important as those of the abuse survivor. On the other hand, the abuse survivor is really sick at times, and needs some help when they're sick (but not help from the kids). How do you handle all this?

What Is NOT Your Responsibility

Well, first of all, it's *not* up to you to handle it all. It's up to the abuse survivor to make their best effort at recovering, and they have *full responsibility* for their problem. But there are times they'll need your help or help from a professional. So you need only be concerned with learning about the illness, and helping when possible. It's not up to you to cure it, or to take responsibility for the sufferer's happiness. And you and your children must be able to live your own lives.

The sufferer should want that for all of you. I assume he/she loves you all, and wants you to be happy. His/her illness is not intentional, or meant to hurt anyone. That's good to keep in mind when things get a little rough.

Why Is This Happening?

Depression and PTSD are hard to handle. There's sadness, negativity, and outbursts of anger, and they often don't make sense—not to other people, or even to the sufferer. Why is your loved one living in this personal hell? Why do they sometimes behave so irrationally, and why are they sometimes so angry?

If you've read this book so far, you know it's because they were abused. And you may have begun to understand what that abuse did to their feelings about themselves and others. You know more about why they have depression and PTSD. And how they feel when they are sick. *The more you understand about these things, the better for all of you.* When you can help, that makes recovery more likely. So you don't want to *hide* from the problem, you want to *learn* as much about it as you can.

Your Feelings Are Important

You can't forget or push aside your own feelings. You may feel a need for help from a therapist too, and that can be a good idea (if the therapist is good and understands PTSD, and perhaps family therapy). Just remember that it can be hard to find a good therapist, and you don't want an incompetent person added to the mix! You can look carefully and go a step at a time until you're sure you can trust the therapist not to harm you or your family (like some of mine did—but there *were* a couple of good ones). Sometimes it may be good for the whole family to get help from a family therapist.

There's nothing that will help more, than all of you developing good communication skills. In such an atmosphere, everyone's feelings are considered, and problems are worked out. We've talked about how to do this, and a good family therapist knows how to do this.

PTSD is hard to deal with, because the sufferer *is in a past emotional reality*. Their *feelings* are telling them that you, and maybe your children, are abusing them the way they were actually abused as a child. That can make you the focus for anger, fears, suspicion, and other strong feelings appropriate only toward the abusing parent. This is very upsetting and confusing to all involved (the sufferer will not understand it either, until he learns about it). Only knowledge and understanding can overcome this, and that takes time and a lot of hard work.

Things To Keep In Mind And Things You Can Do

A few things to keep in mind are:

- *It's not about you, you didn't do anything wrong* (unintentionally triggering PTSD is an innocent mistake, and is not "doing something wrong").

- *You can gently encourage and support* good therapy and/or medication for your spouse, or family therapy, if they can accept that.

- *You can learn* what triggers the PTSD, so you can help avoid triggers.

- *The sufferer is not faking*. They are in a past reality. They need to learn how to get back to the present, and you can help them do this. Their disorder is not an insult to you, or something intentional. It is an *automatic* mental/emotional process caused by their abuse.

- *There will be things you can learn to say (or not say)* that will avoid more triggering and help the sufferer get back to the present. "You're a good person", and other words that counter what an abused person feels, can help. You can try to avoid criticising, threatening or manipulating. And don't push if they can't handle something right now.

- *It can help for the spouse to say* "I'm sorry I hurt you, and I promise I'll try my best not to say/do that again". That's not because you've done something wrong. It's because they need to hear this in that moment.

- *Think of saying that as a gift.* At that moment, the sufferer is in great pain, and their greatest fear is that you will do the trigger again, on and on forever (like the abuser did). It feels like the pain will never go away. This doesn't mean you're taking responsibility. You're just reassuring them that you won't intentionally hurt them (and doing this helps separate you from the abusing parent in the victim's mind).

- *Some physical displays of affection*, such as hugging, back rub, foot massage, etc. can help if it's O.K. with the sufferer. If they're not ready, you can wait and try later, if you want to.

- *To get past PTSD*, the sufferer has to see and feel that the spouse (or child, etc.) and the abuser are *not* the same person. The more they see that the triggering is an accident, and that you love them and care about them, the easier and quicker it will be to return to normal. While you can help, *they* have to do most of this.

- *PTSD really shakes up the sufferer*. It may go right on into deep depression. Afterwards, I've sometimes felt that my feet weren't quite on solid ground, sometimes for a few days. Just try not to be too demanding, and give them some time to get over it.

- *The faster both of you can shut PTSD down*, the less severe it will be, and the less likely there will be deep depression afterward.

What You're Likely To Feel

You will likely feel negative emotions, such as anger, guilt, etc. These feelings are natural and important to you. Unfortunately, *the person in PTSD will be blind to them* **temporarily**, and it will do no good to try to share them at this time (once the storm is over, sharing will be possible). Try not to give in to these feelings, and remain as positive as you can. This is not an easy thing to do.

But the sufferer *can't* help you while in PTSD, and a negative response on your part will only make things worse for everyone. No, it's not fair, but when someone is in the throes of illness, fair doesn't always work.

Try to wait until the sufferer is back to normal. Then you can discuss your feelings in a positive way. If you come on too negative, it may trigger the sufferer again, which is bad for all of you. You could consider this another gift to your spouse, who is suffering at the moment and is unable to attend to your needs. Your feelings are just as important.

After an episode, the sufferer is likely to feel guilt and remorse and will want to make it up to you. *Just don't add more to the guilt.* That could be another trigger. If you can't find a good way to discuss your feelings later, consider seeking the help of a good family therapist. *Your feelings are just as important as the sufferer's.*

And Then There's Depression

Deep depression is also hard to deal with, and there isn't much you can do but listen and be positive yourself. Try not to lose patience. It's stressful to have someone so negative (while depressed) around. *One help for this can be medication for the sufferer.* Be sure to do some things that make you feel good, and take care of yourself. This will give you more strength to deal with it.

If the sufferer shows any sign of suicidal urges, insist they get help **right away**. This is very dangerous. You are not responsible if the sufferer harms himself. That would be caused by the illness. Just use common sense, and treat it as an emergency.

Some things you may feel when the sufferer is in PTSD are:

- *Anger over being "attacked"*. The sufferer is *actually* feeling the need to defend himself against you (as the person who *appears* to be the old abuser), and against the PTSD, which is an avalanche of intense pain. They may not understand why you feel attacked (they will be able to when they get out of PTSD). They may perceive your reasonable feelings as another attack on them, while they're still in the disorder.

- *Confusion*, because it all seems so unreal (which it is).

- *Guilt* over "causing" pain. This is an accident. The pain is caused by the abuser(s), not you. If you're trying your best to help, you're doing enough.

- *Being trapped in a nightmare*. This is true as long as any of the participants is not trying to fix the problem. If everyone keeps trying, you're *not* trapped, and the nightmare *will* go away. Meanwhile, you need to try to enjoy life and take care of yourself.

What About The Children? Bad Things Can Happen

There are some dangers to the children of victims of child abuse. One is the possibility of their being abused the way their parent was. But even where the abuse victim swears they will not harm their children, some bad things can happen. If PTSD is present, the child may trigger it, and feel the wrath of their parent's rage. Or they may see crushing depression, or hear talk of suicide. These things can be big problems for a child.

The child may develop anger problems, or they may feel responsible for the parent's feelings. Or they may be confused by the parent's two–sidedness. This can cause low self–esteem, and/or the need to rescue or take care of others, including the parent. It can also cause them to withdraw from the parent. These things are not good for a child's development.

In the last chapter we talked about when there is real danger to the child, and things the family can do when there is not. Assuming you can work on this as a family, what does the child need to know? And what should you not burden them with?

Let Them Know They Didn't Cause This

The child needs to know that they are not responsible *in any way* for the illness. The sufferer should *always* apologize to their child if they've hurt them. They should make it as clear as possible that *"It's not you, it's me"*, and that dad/mom has an illness that they are trying hard to fix.

Also make clear that the child is not at fault, and didn't cause the illness or pain, and that *they* can't fix it. You could ask that the child try to avoid saying or doing certain things (triggers), *if* they can understand. If they can't, you shouldn't expect their help. They are the kids, and it's yours and the sufferer"s job to take care of them, regardless of what problems you have. It's reasonable to expect a child to try not to hurt someone, but they can't be held in any way responsible for the sufferer's illness or pain.

They Need Both Their Parents

The spouse needs to be careful not to shut down the relationship between the sufferer and their child, in the name of protecting the child (as long as the child is safe). Not allowing abuse is definitely right, but branding the sufferer as unworthy of a real relationship is not. The sufferer and the child need to be trusted to relate in their own way, as long as the sufferer is not abusing (Sexual abuse is a different story. If this has happened, any relationship or contact must always be carefully monitored.).

The child needs and loves both parents, and there should be room for this to work out, if it is safe. The spouse should not try to run or over–monitor this relationship, as long as the sufferer is not abusing the child. As the sufferer recovers, things will get much better.

Here's How The Sufferer Can Be Involved In Their Lives

For their part, the sufferer needs to show the child love, spend time with them, and get involved by showing interest in what the child feels and is doing. Build something or do something together. Play the child's favorite games with them. Read to them when they are young. Share a hobby.

Be a school chaperone, or support interests like baseball, Biology, or whatever they care about. Lots of love and involvement will show the child how it really is. *When you are able*, let the child tell you how your disorder made them feel, including specific incidents. Don't spare the hugs and kisses. And don't be afraid to say you're sorry.

To The Sufferer: Just Do Your Best

One of the hardest things about this problem is knowing that you may have hurt a loved one. I think if you do your best and try hard to be a loving family member, and do your best to heal and recover, things will work out well. As you get better, these problems will fade. People know you by who you are most of the time, not by your occasional failures and mistakes. The mark of good character is that you try hard and never quit trying. And healthy people are imperfect, too.

And now for my final topic: To forgive, or not to forgive the abusing parent(s).

Chapter Twenty-Two

You And Your Abusing Parent

Until you achieve healing and recovery, your adult relationship with your abusing parent(s) is likely to be an up and down kind of thing—mostly down. However much you may try to have things be normal between you, sooner or later the conflicts will come out, and the anger and pain will return. While healing and recovery is taking place, it's not easy for any of you to understand what's happening. At this point, things are in flux, and nothing is very clear. That will change after recovery.

In This, You Come First

One thing I'm sure about. *You have to put yourself and your recovery first*. You can't even think to improve this relationship until you've gone through the recovery, especially the part where you get familiar with your anger, and also when you stand up to them.

I had to learn how to be myself, and to stand up for myself, before these relationships could change. If you try to rush or gloss over this, you are likely to go backwards. You can't recover if you are worried about your abuser(s), no matter how much you may love them.

One reason is that you have to see clearly *just what they did to you, and the effect it has had on you,* before you can heal. If you're too worried about how they'll feel about that, you can't do it the way you need to. If there's any hope of a real relationship, they will have to know and begin to understand the full import of what they did to you. And they will have to somehow sincerely apologize for it (some people speak more with actions than with words).

That may or may not happen. If it does happen, it may take a long time. If you're going to worry about that, you will never get around to healing yourself, and recovering from what happened.

You Have To Be Willing To Let Them Go

You have to be willing to let them go, if that's what it takes. I remember feeling after my "standing up" that I might never see my parents again. While that was painfully sad, I also felt relieved of a great burden for the first time. I didn't know what would happen. I had always loved my parents, so part of the feeling was grief. I wasn't at all sure that they loved me enough to want me to heal from what they had done. I grieved for weeks afterward, and waited.

There is no way for you to know what will happen in this situation. That depends on what *they* are capable of, and has nothing to do with you. *You can't control this*, and you just have to wait to see what happens. I was fortunate that my parents chose to keep trying, and we developed a loving family relationship afterward. But to fully recover, I had to be willing to take the chance that it would *not* work out. If that had been the case, I would have lived with it. You have to stand up for yourself, and keep standing up if you want to recover.

You have to be willing to go on without them, if necessary.

To Forgive Or Not Forgive

Here's where you will definitely get lots of advice. Some will say you have to forgive, or you'll be bitter and that will eat at you. Some will say, Never! I found the truth to be somewhere in–between. As I've said above, *you can't be concerned with your abusing parent(s) while you are recovering*, or that will stop your recovery. The same goes for forgiveness.

You Can't Forgive Until...

Until you've gotten in touch with your intense childhood anger, how could it help to forgive your parent(s)? That would not only be premature, but would likely make you skip that very important step in healing. The same is true about standing up. How could you do an effective standing up if you forgive your parent(s) first? Not possible! *Premature* forgiveness, because it's supposedly "The right thing to do", will stop your recovery.

It Will Happen When You're Ready, And Not Before

After you complete the key points of your recovery, forgiveness will be a natural thing that comes out of your increasing knowledge and confidence. As you recover, you will understand more about why your parents behaved as they did. The more you understand their circumstances, the more you'll know why the abuse happened. You may come to think as I do, that most people do what they think is their best, and what they think is right. How one can think its O. K. to abuse a child is a little complicated. It involves people fooling themselves into justifying taking out their feelings on an innocent child. It involves a kind of immaturity, and there is very often the fact that they were also abused as a child.

Some Will See, Some Will Not

Bottom line: Your abusing parent can love you (or not) *and* abuse you. What will matter in the long run is whether they can see that they did wrong. Some will, and some won't.

After Recovery, You Will Probably Forgive—And Move On

But when we have recovered and know the whole truth (why your parent was incapable of giving you what you needed), it's possible to love and forgive the abuser, whether they are able to see they did wrong or not. Whether they return your love or not. Whether you will see them again or not. When you can do that, you have not only healed and recovered, you have moved on!

It's Complicated, And Human

It's common to portray abusers as monsters, or as evil people. That makes it easier to distance oneself from them ("I could never do those awful things!"), but usually it's not true. Some abusers can be otherwise good people. They may have just been primed to abuse you by being abused themselves. And perhaps the easiest thing to do was to just let it happen (a weakness of character). There are so many ways an abuser can justify what they're doing, and believe it's the right thing to do.

We humans are very good at fooling ourselves when we really need to. It can be any excuse from "discipline" to blaming the child for your unhappiness. When you're somehow driven from within to do this, there will always be a "good reason" you can find for it.

The truth is just not simple. Really nasty people can do it. Good people who love their kids can do it. It's just something that happens to some people, and in different ways. It's part of the human tragedy/comedy.

The good news, as I have learned, is that when people really try to overcome this, they can. It starts with a choice made by at least two people, and maybe requires some strength of character. If I could recover, so can many (not all) other people. And if my family could come together in love after this, so can some (not all) other families. These are choices *some* people can make.

Advice For The Abuser What Your Child Needs Most

If you are one of those who loves their child, yet have abused them, I have some advice for you. If you have been denying what happened, but know it is true, you may be scared about what will happen if you admit to it. You may have other fears of your own, and it's very possible you were abused yourself as a child. Just know that two things your child needs badly from you are 1) *a sincere apology*, and 2) *to be told that you love them*. These two things will mean a great deal to your child if you can do them. You may have to do this *many* times, and it may take some time for them to believe you.

It may be hard for them to trust you after what happened, but it's not impossible (because they probably want to).

You Can Recover Too—And Apology Is Good

If you (abuser) were also abused, that has left scars on you also, and has caused you problems. If so, then you too can try to heal and recover. If you can give love and apologies to your adult child, they may turn out to become a real friend, and the love may come back to you multiplied. That's one reason it's worth the risk.

How much should you apologize? *As much as it takes* until your child really believes it. It will be over when it's over for them. And as I found out, it sometimes does get to be over.

Guilt May Be Real, But Need Not Be Overwhelming

You will probably feel some guilt, which is appropriate *up to a point*. But you should not be overwhelmed by this guilt. If you are sorry for what you did wrong, and want to do right by your child now, that is enough. You likely have problems of your own, and to the extent that it is possible for you, get some good help for these problems. You can't change the past, but you can change the present and the future. We all have the power to decide to change ourselves, and the way we behave toward others. Once that decision is made, change begins.

It's Worth Trying

It is my belief that the love people share between them is the best thing in this life, and the only thing that lasts, even beyond death. Whatever your fears or reservations, they are not as important as the love that may be possible between you and your child. That's why it's worth doing whatever it takes to nurture and preserve it. I say go for it.

Best Wishes

So, dear reader—I hope you'll make the choice to heal and recover. I'm here to tell you it's possible, it can be done. That's why I've shared with you what I have learned over these many years. So you can look at my experience, and gain ideas for your own unique approach to recovery.

We're all different in some ways, and we're the same in some ways. The things I did to recover may not all be what you need to do. But at the very least, they can give you new ideas. Then you can find your own path. If nothing else, I'm proof that it's not hopeless, and that it can be done!

Now, let's review some important points about recovery.

Chapter Twenty-Three

The Foundations Of Recovery

It's time now to summarize what I've told you, and give an outline of the recovery process, as I see it. Hopefully this will help you put things in perspective for working out your own recovery plan. I'll mark things that I think were key to my recovery with a (K).

Attitudes That Lead To Success

- A willingness to take full responsibility for yourself and your problems (K)

- An understanding that we are all different, and we have to find our own way

- A strong determination to work things out

- A dedication to follow the truth, wherever it might lead

- A commitment to do the right thing, whatever you perceive it to be (K)

- A desire to understand the reasons for your problems

- The courage and determination to face and handle sometimes overwhelming emotional pain

- A willingness to seek and accept help (K)

- A determination to live your own life, in your own way

- A determination not to give up until you succeed, no matter what (K)

The Need For Good Help

You'll need a good helper (K)—you can't do it all by yourself. That's because *some parts of recovery, like working on your defenses, are dangerous without a trained, competent helper*. From my experience, finding the right helper is likely to take more than one try. So you have to be prepared to keep trying when a therapist doesn't work out. It's also likely that you may gain something positive from a therapist who can't help you all the way through, so it won't be a total loss. If you are realistic and persistent, all will work out well.

Suicidal Urges Are An Emergency!

If you are having suicidal urges, you **must** deal with that right away. If the helper you turn to is not helping, *immediately* seek another, and don't blame yourself. Continue to seek and then to be treated until the urges are gone, and the depression is under control. If these things come back, *get help again.* As you recover, you will come to understand why you had suicidal urges, and you'll be glad you stuck around for what is likely to be the best part of your life.

It's Not Your Fault

An important part of my recovery was learning—and coming to really believe—that none of the abuse was my fault (K). Most of those abused as children believe it is their fault, because of how we see our parents when we are very young.

We Kings And Queens Of Denial

Denial and other defenses are wired into our psyches, and it's natural that we try to use them when we run into trouble. But for people with serious problems, like being an abuse survivor, these defenses not only don't work, but can become obstacles to recovery. They do this when they keep us from getting the help we need, and when they make us afraid to admit we have a problem. The sooner we get past these defenses, the sooner we begin to recover (K). *Warning!* Defenses can be like the structural elements of a building. If you pull them down without providing a substitute, the building will fall. That's why you need the help of a good trained professional if you are stuck in your defenses.

Understanding The Reasons For Your Problems

Learning the reasons for your feelings and behavior (K) is an important part of recovery, and this takes time. Most important are hidden anger (K) and fear (K). Science tells us that there is a reason for everything. And that all these reasons, while some are not yet known, *can* one day be known.

You can learn enough of these reasons to understand who you are and how you got that way. Then you can learn to love and accept yourself, just the way you are, which is *unconditional love* (K). Once you learn to love yourself unconditionally, you'll be more able to love others that way.

You'll also be able to have better relationships and outcomes in all parts of your life, once you learn to stop continuing to abuse yourself. And you'll come to see yourself as a good person, who deserves to enjoy living life *your own* way.

This doesn't mean you have to *like* all your feelings and behaviors. It's good to want to change them if they make you unhappy, or cause problems. But it's much easier to change things you *don't like* about yourself when you love yourself unconditionally. It's a more self–tolerant and less frantic process, and is positively motivated, which means it's more likely to succeed.

Using Medications When Prescribed

Many times, as in my case, anti–depressant medications, used under medical advice and supervision, can elevate or stabilize your moods to the point that you have much more energy to use for your recovery, and for your life in general (K). It's possible to find one at a dose that helps, but does not cause unpleasant side effects.

You must consult a trusted physician to supervise this. Sometimes people feel that taking medication is admitting a weakness. But is that really a good reason to avoid getting better?

I also found that propranolol helped me with anxiety. You can ask your physician what is right or safe for you.

My experience is to be wary of tranquilizers, especially when used for depression or PTSD on a daily basis. Only take these when your physician recommends it, and can explain how they will help you.

"Standing Up" Can Make You More Free

Standing up to the abuser, when done right, is one of the most powerful steps to recovery. In it, you stand up for yourself in an adult way, something you could never have done as a child. A successful standing up can change how you feel about yourself, and how you relate to your abuser (K). It really has to be done right to work (have a therapist help you), and the changes will last the rest of your life.

Be A Good Communicator

Learning this means learning how to listen, and how to be listened to. It will help you learn to accept people as they are, and to accept yourself as you are. Good communicators tend to get along well with others and do well in life.

Learning Your Positive And Negative Ways

When you pay attention to your negative thoughts, you can learn why you do this, and develop a more positive outlook. And learning the power of positive thinking and attitudes, and how to use that power, can turn your life around (K). This leads directly to more positive things happening in your life, and helps your recovery. I found that this was a *very important* step. Then you follow with positive goals, and soon your life is changing the way you want it to.

Being Part Of The Lives Of Those You Love

Some things I had to learn were how my abuse and resultant PTSD affected my relationships with others (K). Once I learned what had happened and what to look out for, my relationships all improved.

As I progressed in my recovery, I became more involved in the lives of those I love, and found that I could be there more when they needed me. At the same time, I found that I was living life more my own way, and getting more out of it. Oddly enough, *as we become fuller in ourselves, we have more to give when we want to*. Giving is not an act of submission, but a joyful act of love.

What Can You Expect?

How long does recovery take? *I can only guess* how much my own 30-year-plus recovery would have speeded up had I known all these things when I started. I think you'd see significant results early on, and some big changes within a year. "Full" recovery (you never really stop) might take a few years or more (just a guess). If you think that's long, think of how long it took me. Most of my life! I'd have given a lot to cut my recovery time to a few years!

You probably won't have to see your therapist all that time, as each major step will require you to do a lot of the work on your own. After "banging my head against the wall" with therapy attempts for many, many years, it only took a few sessions with my best therapist to be in the home stretch. So it probably won't cost a fortune (Whoops! There goes another excuse not to get moving.).

Finally, I wish you my very best in your recovery efforts. I've now told you all I know to this point about *my* recovery, and I'm sure you will probably be able to teach me a few things by the time you complete yours. Good luck in all your endeavors!

Appendix

How The Science Needs To Improve

Treatment Standards

When you go to a medical doctor, you have to be careful, but you can expect standard treatment backed by the latest scientific evidence. All doctors will treat you in *basically* the same way. They will weigh and measure you, and take your blood pressure and pulse. They will mostly order the same tests and prescribe the same drugs for the same symptoms. Why is it different for Psychiatry and Psychology, where one therapist may do one thing, and another does something entirely different? Literally anything seems to go, according to how the therapist was trained, and sometimes it can seem random. I think this is very confusing to patients and clients, and I think it makes the therapist's job harder and more stressful. I believe the problem here is a lack of basic treatment standards.

In the social sciences, you have widely differing "frameworks", or "schools of thought". There is everything from Freudianism to behaviorism, transactional to "reality" therapy and beyond. And they are all very different. Your therapist may subscribe to one of these, or some combination of them. *You do not know what you are getting if the therapist doesn't tell you.* This can lead as much to failure as to success.

To make matters worse, there sometimes seems to be a kind of religious zealotry in these various schools, with the founders referred to as "the master" (Freud) or just worshipped as a hero or guru. Unfortunately, *religion or belief has no place in science.* Science is just *the latest, best approximation of the truth,* based on data obtained by use of the scientific method.

One way to help correct this problem would be for the major professional associations to adopt *voluntary* treatment standards that all can agree on, based on the latest science. This would allow patients/clients and therapists to know more what to expect of each other, and of the therapy itself. This would lead, I think, to more success, and to less avoidance of therapy. When everyone knows what's coming, it's easier to prepare for it, less scary, and more efficient.

Some examples: A fairly standard assessment procedure. Probing strengths as well as weaknesses. Recognizing the limitations of diagnostic labels. Clear disclosure of therapeutic methods used. Focusing on the patient's goals and timely needs. Accepting the obligation to refer when therapy is not working.

The Scientific Method And The Social Sciences

I think the problem here is that in the physical sciences, we are observing things happening outside our minds, but in the social sciences *we are using our minds to observe our minds*. And in our minds are *beliefs and personal experience, plus personal emotions.* This creates *biases* that are so far not accounted for in the scientific method, which was originally designed for observing the *physical* world.

As for the weakness I see in the scientific method, we'd somehow have to keep our mental biases from contaminating research models and rendering experimental results useless. One way would be to include scientists from at least two or more frameworks in designing experiments. Their agreement on methodology would go a long way toward eliminating the problem of the biased mind making pre–conclusions about the mind.